CREATING NEW HABITS

Learn How To Break Bad Habits, Use Goal Setting And Why Willpower Won't Work

JACK THOMAS

© **Copyright 2020 - All rights reserved.**

The content contained within this book may not be reproduced, duplicated or transmitted without direct written permission from the author or the publisher.

Under no circumstances will any blame or legal responsibility be held against the publisher, or author, for any damages, reparation, or monetary loss due to the information contained within this book, either directly or indirectly.

Legal Notice:

This book is copyright protected. It is only for personal use. You cannot amend, distribute, sell, use, quote or paraphrase any part, or the content within this book, without the consent of the author or publisher.

Disclaimer Notice:

Please note the information contained within this document is for educational and entertainment purposes only. All effort has been executed to present accurate, up to date, reliable, complete information. No warranties of any kind are declared or implied. Readers acknowledge that the author is not engaged in the rendering of legal, financial, medical or professional advice. The content within this book has been derived from various sources. Please consult a licensed professional before attempting any techniques outlined in this book.

By reading this document, the reader agrees that under no circumstances is the author responsible for any losses, direct or indirect, that are incurred as a result of the use of the information contained within this document, including, but not limited to, errors, omissions, or inaccuracies.

Contents

Introduction	vii
1. WHAT IS A HABIT?	1
Why Are They Formed?	8
Why Do We Have Bad Habits?	13
2. THE HABIT LOOP	18
The Routine	22
The Reward	27
3. WHY WILLPOWER WON'T WORK	32
The Research	36
The Myth of Self-Control	40
4. THE IMPORTANCE OF A GOAL	46
How to Set Goals	50
The Power of Intention	54
5. CHANGING YOUR HABITS	60
The 3-Step Process	64
Step One: Awareness Training	65
Step Two: Why Do You Do It?	66
Step Three: The Reward	68
6. EXPERIMENT WITH NEW ROUTINES	73
Example Routines for Addictive Habits	77
Give It Time	81
7. BE CONSISTENT	86
When Does A Habit Become a Habit?	90
It's All About Repetition	94

8. THE KEY INGREDIENT · 99

   Conclusion · 105
   References · 109

Introduction

Breaking bad habits can be difficult. Ask anyone who's tried. Quite often, we don't even know what our bad habits are, or are unaware of them until they do some real damage to our health, relationships, and lifestyles. Reaching for something sweet after dinner, biting our nails when we are stressed, turning the TV on as soon as we get home from work — all of these are things we do unconsciously. When habits take over, they can sometimes consume us, eating away at our health, our social lives, and our productivity.

The solution is to recognize these bad habits and routines and replace them with new ones that are less harmful or even more beneficial to us. With over 10 years of experience studying and working in the social sciences, I've seen over and over how habits can affect our lives. We all have them. As someone who once struggled with a number of bad habits of his own, I can personally vouch for how difficult it is to stop them. Habits are formed in the brain's subconscious, which means that no amount of willpower can stop them alone (Duhigg, 2014). In order to truly beat your bad habits, you first have to understand how they developed in the first place.

Take my own life as an example. My bad habits began with the unhealthy snacking pattern of eating something sweet after every meal. But this wasn't my only habit. In fact, I have a number of good ones, including going to the gym and brushing my teeth every day, and I felt like that was enough to counteract this one bad habit. Then I started watching TV in bed before I fell asleep.

These may sound innocent enough, but before I knew it, they were deeply ingrained in my behavior patterns. The worst of it was that I couldn't even remember how they had started. I would never have even recognized the bad snacking habit for what it was if I hadn't developed the TV habit first. The stimulation from the screen started to negatively affect my sleeping pattern. I'd get a few hours a night of deep sleep (at best), and spent my days in a sleepy daze. Still, I would never have understood how serious my TV watching habit was if I hadn't received a wake-up call in the form of a car accident. The reason? I fell asleep at the wheel.

After the accident, I knew that I had to make a change. Not only was this habit not serving me, but it was destroying my life in ways I had never even realized. Though it felt like a tragedy at the time, this accident put me firmly on a path to discovery. It took me a while to understand how habits work. I tried a number of different methods, but in vain. It was like I was possessed. No matter how disciplined I thought I was, I found myself back in front of the TV after about a week of "quitting." Then something clicked. Once I realized what was truly needed to kick a bad habit, I found myself reading in bed after just a month of applying my newfound strategy. Now, years later, I consistently get 6 hours of sleep a night, and all of the benefits that come with it. How did I finally manage to kick this habit (and so quickly)? That method is what this book is all about.

Not only will this book provide you with a real, practical plan for changing bad habits, it will teach you how they form in the brain so that you can transform your destructive habits into ones that serve you better. Habit formation has increasingly become a topic of focused study, especially as advances are made in the fields of cognitive science. Throughout the years, I have used this research, tweaked and perfected the method that I once used to kick my TV watching habit, and all of the advice I present to you in this book is based on recent studies and grounded in accepted scientific knowledge.

By the time you've finished reading this book, you will be able to identify many of your own habits (including some that you didn't realize you had), as well as determine which ones are serving you and

Introduction

which ones need to be transformed into something better. If you are committed enough and follow the simple techniques outlined here, there is no reason why you, too, can't stop that bad habit that has been plaguing you for years.

The longer you have a bad habit, the more it will begin to affect your life, and the harder it will be to break. As such, time is a critical component of habit formation. The longer you wait to tackle your bad habits, the harder it will be to overcome them.

The time to break your bad habits is right now. With this book to guide you, you will have all of the resources you need to tackle that habit that has been negatively affecting your life. Better still, you'll come away from this book with the tools to transform that habit into something that will improve your life in the long run. This book will provide you with the latest scientific research, as well as practical tips and actionable advice to help you get started as soon as possible. You no longer have to live at the mercy of your subconscious. No matter what habit you're struggling with or how long you've struggled, you now have the power to change and take back control over your own life and your own happiness.

Bad habits can make us feel utterly helpless. Worse, it can make us feel crazy, especially when they seem unbreakable. How can we claim to be in control of our own lives when we can't even do something as simple as turn off the TV at night or limit the number of cookies we eat? This book will help you understand

Introduction

that habits, good or bad, are a natural part of the way that our brains work. You're not crazy, and you no longer have to feel helpless. If you're ready to take back control of your life, then you've come to the right place.

1

What is a Habit?

As far back as 1892, William James wrote, "All our life, so far as it has definite form, is but a mass of habits." More than 100 years later, modern psychology and neuroscience has only proven him correct. We are very good at rationalizing the choices we make throughout the day, convincing ourselves that our actions are the product of well-thought-out reasoning. But the reality is very different. Most of our choices are not conscious, but habitual. A 2006 study conducted by Duke University even found that more than 40% of the daily actions performed by participants were habitual, rather than conscious choices (Schmidt & Retelsdorf, 2016). While each individual habit may not seem like much, they ultimately pile on top of one another to form a huge part of our lifestyles, well-being, and even, to a certain extent, our personalities. Habits inform the meals we order, the things we say to our children every night, our likelihood to spend or save money, how often we exercise, the ways in which we organize our work routines, and even the ways in which we organize our thoughts. Habits are things that we rarely think too much about until one of them starts to compromise our health, productivity, financial security, or happiness in a serious way (Schmidt & Retelsdorf, 2016).

Anyone who's tried to quit a bad habit or form a new, beneficial habit can testify to how difficult it is. At times, it can feel impossible. Many people struggle for years to give up unhealthy habits or to start new ones, but no amount of willpower seems to make it happen. At the same time, we see countless examples of people who successfully quit chemical addictions like smoking or drinking, or who woke up one morning and decided they were going to run four miles every day. All of us who have struggled to change our own habits have seen someone successfully change theirs. So, what is the secret?

To learn this, a team of researchers in Bethesda, Maryland, conducted a year's long study of people from all demographics and across several different countries who had successfully and dramatically changed their lives by overcoming one destructive habit (Duhigg, 2014). People in the study had managed to quit smoking, drinking, overeating, and obsessive shopping, just to list a few. What the researchers wanted to know was how habits worked on a chemical, neurological level (Duhigg, 2014). When these people overcame their habits, did anything change about the way that their brains work? Are some people just cognitively more equipped to start and stop bad habits than others?

What these researchers found was that almost every participant in the study had managed to overcome their destructive habits by replacing them with ones that were beneficial. They didn't simply stop smoking or shopping — they replaced these habits with something else, something better like jogging or reading. These changes were actually visible in brain scans. The old sets of neurological patterns, the ones that instigated the old habits, were overwritten by new ones. The researchers could still see the workings and occasionally firing up of the old pathways, especially when participants were exposed to triggers like going to a party with alcohol or eating a big meal at a fancy restaurant. However, those pathways were clogged up and crowded out by the new patterns, the replacement habits that had been formed to "cure" those impulses. In short, this study shows us that habits do indeed come from deep within our brains, and that when even one habit changes, it's enough to reroute entire sections of our brains.

Destructive habits like overeating or excess shopping cause us a severe amount of emotional, social, and even physical distress (Chen et al., 2020). It's this distress that causes us to notice them in the first place. What we rarely consider are all of the many little habits that aren't causing us distress — at least, not yet. Think about your own day today. What did you do first when you got up in the morning? Perhaps you went straight into the shower, grabbed your phone to check your email, or went into the kitchen to make yourself a bagel. Did you brush your teeth before or after your morning shower? When you put on your shoes, did you tie the left one or the right one first? On your way to work, what did you say to your partner or children? Which route did you take to work? And when you arrived at work, what was the first thing you did? Did you fire up your office computer to check your emails, spend a few minutes chatting with colleagues in the locker room, or start right in on today's project? What did you eat for lunch? When you got home, did you change your sneakers to go for your run, or did you grab a beer from the fridge and turn on the TV?

Whatever your answers are to these questions, chances are they would be almost exactly the same if I asked you tomorrow, or the day after. Chances are that your answers would have been the same if I asked you three months ago, or even three years ago. These and so many other decisions aren't consciously made. We do them almost automatically. We don't spend time in the morning consciously deciding which shoe to tie, nor do we carefully plan out the words we're going to use to say good-bye to our partners or roommates. All of these actions and more are habits, ones that develop slowly but surely over the course of our lives (Sims, 2018).

Human brains developed the capacity for habit

building, but it's only very recently that scientists have been able to observe habitual activity in the brain (Wood & Rünger, 2016). As it turns out, understanding how habits work is the key to making or breaking them. Once you understand what habits are and how they work in the brain, you'll be much better able to change the ones that aren't serving you into ones that will.

The commonly accepted scientific definition of habits is "learned sequences of acts that have become automatic responses to specific cues, and are functional in obtaining certain goals or end states." In other words, habits are certain behaviors that we do over and over again until they become automatic (Wood & Rünger, 2016). The first time you set your alarm to ring at 6am, it was a conscious choice. But after waking up at 6am every single day for three years, you probably find that you're waking up at 6am even on the weekends.

The most important part of this definition, however, is the last part. Habits don't become habits if they aren't beneficial in some way (Ainslie, 2016). If waking up at 6am wasn't rewarding, you would start waking up earlier or later. If you smacked your elbow on the door the first time you went to tie your right shoe, you'd probably start tying your left shoe first. Habits (even bad ones) are formed because they make us feel good. And if there are no immediate negative consequences, then we keep repeating that behavior that rewarded us over and over again until it becomes automatic. This is great for behaviors like brushing your teeth or going to the gym three nights a week, but it's not great for behaviors like watching TV in bed or smoking a cigarette after you eat. Sure, watching TV in bed isn't good for you, but it *feels* good. And one night of TV watching won't disrupt your sleeping patterns that much. As it turns out, a few weeks of TV watching won't disrupt your sleeping patterns that much either, and so you do it every single night until it becomes a habit. It only becomes a "bad" habit when it *does* start to impact your sleeping patterns, but at that point you're unable to stop. Watching TV is no longer a conscious choice. It's something that you've quite literally programmed your brain to do.

The online Oxford dictionary tells us that a habit is "a settled or regular tendency or practice, especially one that is hard to give up," as well as "an automatic reaction to a specific situation." Though the dictionary lists these as two different definitions, both are true (Chen et al., 2020). Habits often begin as reactions to specific circumstances or life situations. You come home from work exhausted one night, so you decide to watch TV instead of going for a run. After a few nights or even a few weeks of this, you start watching TV when you come home from work no matter how your work day went. What began as a solution to a specific, situational problem has become an automatic reaction to the situation itself. Once it becomes automatic, it does indeed become difficult to give up.

There are three things that must happen before a specific action becomes a habit. First, it has to be successfully repeated over and over again. Nothing becomes a habit after just doing it just once or twice. It's only after repeating a behavior many times that it starts to become automatic. Second, the habit has to satisfy some kind of identity or self-image marker. Habits are how we organize our lives, and so a behavior that obviously contradicts our self-image is unlikely to become a habit. Where this becomes tricky, however, is that the person that we consciously want to be isn't always the person that we subconsciously want to be. For example, you may have done a great job convincing yourself that you want to be a world-class surgeon, but if, deep down, your heart isn't in it, that will start to crop up in your habits. You may start ignoring your pages or find it difficult to get out of bed in the morning. You might find yourself cutting corners on your paperwork or drinking extra sugary coffees in the morning to combat the stress of the job. Often, the "rewards" that habits give us are nothing more than a brief respite from tasks that we consider unpleasant or that we really don't want to do, regardless of what our conscious minds are telling us.

Finally, in order for something to be considered a habit it has to be a behavior that's automatic. This is measured first by a lack of awareness. If you find yourself reaching up to adjust your glasses while you're wearing contacts, you'll experience a moment of discomfort as your fingers search for frames that aren't there. Until you experience this discomfort, you may not have even realized how often you adjust your glasses. You perform this action without being aware of it at all. Second, automaticity is measured by the amount of control (or lack thereof) you have over a certain action. You may think you have the fortitude to skip dessert tonight. But do you have the fortitude to skip every night? When you find yourself engaged in a battle of wills with yourself, you're encountering a process that's become automatized, to some degree, inside your brain.

Why Are They Formed?

Why would our brains evolve to automatize certain actions? Is this function simply a neurological accident?

Perhaps, but many studies suggest that habits form in the brain to free up cognitive ability to focus and think critically (Wood, 2017). Imagine how difficult it would be to get through the morning if you had to consciously remind yourself to brush your teeth or tie your shoes. The more your routine actions become automatically programmed, the more energy and ability you have to think about more important things. The time that you *don't* spend thinking about when to brush your teeth can be devoted to mentally reviewing the notes you took for today's big test or planning what you're going to wear to your date tonight.

The actions that ultimately become habits aren't accidental, either. Almost every single action that becomes a habit starts as a conscious choice that helps you fulfill a certain goal. That goal can be vague or specific, big or small. For example, the habit of taking a shower every day serves the big, vague goal of having good hygiene. The habit of opening up a beer when you get home from work, on the other hand, serves the small, specific goal of feeling relaxed after a hard day. The actions that become habits are actions that reward us, and so the automatic programming isn't just about freeing up mental space. It's about encouraging you to repeat actions that had good results, and is intended to prevent you from repeating actions that had bad results.

The problem, however, is that your brain distinguishes "good" and "bad" based on immediate rewards or punishments, rather than on long-term consequences. If a beer makes you feel good in the moment, then your brain encourages you to drink again the following evening. On the other hand, if the very first time you drank you threw up, you'd be much less likely to develop a drinking habit. On the flip side, the first time you go to the gym usually feels terrible. You come out of your workout exhausted and sweaty, with burning muscles and smelly armpits. Though exercise does release a lot of beneficial endorphins in the body, it's not quite enough of an adrenaline rush to make your brain excited for you to get up and go the next morning. In order to make it a habit, you have to exert a lot of discipline in the beginning.

There's one more layer to habit formation that's very important to consider, and that's something that psychologists call "context-response associations" (Wood, 2017). This is what happens when your brain begins to expect certain sensory or emotional results from a specific situation. To illustrate the point, a 2011 experiment looked at the cultural habit of eating popcorn in a movie theater (Wood, 2017). Participants in the theater were randomly given a bag of popcorn that was either freshly made or stale. As you might imagine, most participants reported disliking the stale popcorn. However, the amount of stale popcorn that each participant actually consumed varied greatly according to habit. Those that regularly ate popcorn while watching movies consumed just as much stale popcorn as fresh, while those who weren't habitual popcorn eaters found themselves unable to get through much of the stale popcorn. The association between popcorn snacking and movie watching was so powerful that it overcame the bad taste of the stale popcorn.

Yet, when the exact same participants (with the exact same bags of popcorn) were placed in a conference room and asked to watch music videos, the results were very different. In the lab, no one was able to consume much of the stale popcorn. Even those who were strong popcorn eaters in the movie theater, those who had consumed an entire bag of stale popcorn while watching a movie, were unable to stomach more than a mouthful of stale popcorn in a different context. The basis of their habit was formed, not by rewards or punishments, but by association. They associated eating popcorn with movie theaters. Outside of that context, the compulsion to eat popcorn disappeared.

What this tells us is that understanding *why* we've formed certain habits is just as important as understanding *how* they formed. If your family routinely fights on Thanksgiving, you're going to automatically start feeling tense, edgy, and sensitive around the Thanksgiving table. You've formed an association between Thanksgiving and conflict. You're in the habit of fighting over the Thanksgiving table, even if you consciously, genuinely want to have a peaceful holiday. The habit of snapping over the turkey has certainly not satisfied any goals or given you any rewards. It's a habit formed from context. What would happen if you chose to have Thanksgiving at a different house this year? What if you chose to eat different foods, or gather at a different time? These seemingly arbitrary changes in environment might make all the difference when it comes to circumventing context associated habits.

Whether your habits were created via reward fulfillment or context association (or both), the important thing to remember is that habits have nothing to do with choice. Culturally, we perceive habit formation as something that has to do with character. People with good habits are perceived as being disciplined, motivated, and in control, while people with bad habits are often labeled as lazy, undisciplined, or disorganized, as if they could stop their bad habits at any time. This perception of habits is perhaps the biggest obstacle people face when it comes to making or breaking them. The reality is that habit formation has almost nothing to do with willpower. You can desperately want to do yoga every morning, but getting yourself out of bed 20 minutes early is still going to be difficult. You can clearly understand that spending $100 out of every paycheck on clothes is a problem and still do it. Habits are formed unconsciously, and when they're ingrained enough to truly become "habits," we have very little control over them. The secret to habit transformation is not willpower, it's the opposite. It's about understanding that habit formation is *not* a choice, but rather a complex chemical process that happens slowly over time, often without our awareness.

Why Do We Have Bad Habits?

Let's look at an example. Imagine that you worked a job with long hours. You didn't get home until very late, several hours after your scheduled lunch break. To give yourself an energy boost in the afternoon, you started bringing snacks to work. Slowly but surely, your brain starts to expect a snack in the afternoon. Before you know it, you don't have to think about opening your lunch box—the act of snacking has become a habit. While you're at that job, it's a "good" habit. It gives you an extra dose of energy that you need to get through the working day. It stops you from losing energy or focusing on feelings of hunger. It might even make you less likely to overeat when you get home late at night, as the edge has been taken off your hunger by your afternoon snack. It fulfills the goal of helping you feel energized and satisfied, and it becomes context associated with your office space. You find that you aren't craving snacks on the weekends or on vacation. But when three or four in the afternoon rolls around at work, you find yourself automatically reaching for your lunchbox.

Now imagine that you finally manage to get a new job, one with a better working schedule or maybe one that's closer to where you live. Now you don't get home late anymore. You can have dinner at a more reasonable time. But your afternoon snacking has become a habit. Even though it no longer fulfills the goal of keeping you energized through long working hours, you find yourself unable to repress the urge to eat when three or four o'clock rolls around. Though you're in a different office, you're still sitting in a cubicle doing the same kind of work, and that's enough to make you start craving snacks at a certain time in the afternoon. It doesn't matter if you start to gain weight, or find yourself unable to eat a full meal at dinnertime. You simply can't stop.

Most "bad" habits follow a similar trajectory. They serve a certain purpose at one point in time. They may even be "good" habits when they first start. But a simple change in lifestyle or life circumstances can quickly turn "good" or "harmless" habits into "bad" ones. If you've picked up this book, you are likely in one of two situations: you have a bad habit that you're trying to break, or you have a good habit in mind that you can't seem to start. You know that habits can be unconscious, difficult to spot, and even more difficult to change. Scientific research into the nature of habits aims to understand how and why habits are formed so that we can better understand how to efficiently transform them. Beneficial habits can transform our lives in amazing ways. A daily habit of drinking water or meditating can have beneficial consequences in multiple areas of our lives. Bad habits, on the other hand, can destroy us. Something small and seemingly harmless can wreak a great deal of harm on our mental wellness, physical health, and the quality of our relationships. Understanding the neurology of habit formation will help

Creating New Habits

you to stop feeling powerless to change your own behaviors.

In his book *The Power of Habit*, Charles Duhigg (2014) outlines a process that he calls recognizing our "habit loops." You may be able to identify your bad habits, but recognizing your habit loops will help you to identify what *triggers* those bad habits. Neurologically speaking, you have little to no control over your bad habits, but you have a great deal of control over your triggers. The secret to transforming habits is not learning to change your behaviors as much as it is learning to avoid your triggers. The routines and associations that ultimately lead to your bad habits are the things that need to be changed. If you can change the triggers, then you can stop the habit.

Habit loops occur in three basic steps: cue, routine, and reward. The "cue" is the trigger, the thing that tells your brain it's time to engage in a specific habit. The routine is the behavior or habit itself. And the reward, of course, is the goal that's being fulfilled by this habit.

Identifying your own habit loops can be more difficult than it sounds. Imagine that your bad habit is heading to the cafeteria at lunch and purchasing a sweet from the bakecase. What is your cue? What's the trigger that initiated the formation of this habit in the first place? Is it hunger? Low energy? Or the fact that three of your coworkers also get sweets from the bakecase, and that standing in line with them provides a chance to socialize? Identifying the cue is critical to your success in breaking or transforming this habit. If you are simply hungry, then your attempts to replace that sweet with an apple or a salad would be successful. If your trigger isn't hunger, then the apple just isn't going to satisfy. Your habit wasn't built to satisfy hunger, it was built to satisfy some other need. Until that need or goal is identified, you're going to feel like a zombie in a bad horror movie, compelled to act by some mysterious internal force. Replacing your sweet with something healthy isn't a matter of willpower if hunger isn't the trigger. You can bring apples to work all you want, but once you're exposed to the real cue, then your habit loop will be initiated and you'll be nearly powerless to stop it.

Habits aren't meant to make us feel powerless. If anything, they're meant to empower us. It's our brain's way of programming us to automatically do things that are good for us. Habits are what teach us to be cautious around open flames and put on sunscreen before we go to the beach. Habits like brushing your hair every morning keep you well-groomed. Answering your emails first thing in the morning keeps you organized. Turning off your phone 15 minutes before you go to bed helps you sleep. Because we do these things all the time, and because they're things that coincide with the lifestyles that we want for ourselves, we tend to mistake them for things that are done with intention. It's only when our habit programming goes awry that we start to feel frustrated and powerless. But the same force that prompts you to take out the trash at 8pm is the same force that prompts you to light up a cigarette after lunch. Neither one is a conscious choice. The difference is that one action improves your life, while the other harms it.

The most important lesson behavioral science teaches us about habit is that the stubborn persistence of habitual behaviors has nothing to do with motivation. Being motivated to change is just the first step. But until you've identified your habit loops, you'll find it extremely difficult to modify your behaviors in a lasting way, no matter how dedicated or disciplined you may be.

2

The Habit Loop

All habits follow three specific phases, called the "habit loop." The first phase of the habit loop is called the "cue" or the "trigger." This is a certain situation for which your brain has, over time, programmed a specific behavioral response. That response, of course, is what we call a habit (Chen et. al., 2020).

Psychologists have found that almost all habits are cued by context. There are two forms of environmental habit cues, what psychologists call "direct cueing" and "motivational cueing." Direct cueing is about building relationships between certain routines and certain environments (Chen et. al., 2020). For example, if you always read in the same room or in the same chair, when overtime, you'll find yourself wanting to read whenever you enter that room. You might find it hard to concentrate or study elsewhere, but the mental association between that room and reading automatically preps your brain to concentrate and focus.

Motivational cueing, on the other hand, is about rewards. If drinking coffee in the morning makes you feel more awake, then you're more likely to drink coffee again the next day. If bringing your girlfriend flowers makes her happy, you're more likely to buy her flowers for the next holiday. Actions that produce favorable results (or that don't immediately produce unfavorable results) are more likely to become habits because we're more likely to repeat them.

All habits, good or bad, are triggered by some kind of cue (Chen et. al., 2020). This is how your brain knows that it's time to initiate the habit. Think about your behaviors as mental programs. Your brain stores programmed responses to specific signals. Once your brain gets the signal, it deploys the appropriate program. To create new habits or break old ones, you first need to understand what your cues are, because they aren't always obvious. You might think you drink coffee in the morning because it wakes you up, so you replace coffee with green tea, water, natural energy supplements, a carb based meal — all to no avail. You eventually give up, determining that there's nothing you can do about your coffee habit. But perhaps the energy isn't what cued your coffee drinking after all. What would happen if you put the coffee machine in a different part of the house? Would you go all the way down to the basement or into the living room looking for your cup of coffee? Perhaps your cue is not motivational after all, but direct. The trigger isn't the promise of caffeine, it's the kitchen in the early morning.

In fact, there's a great deal of research to suggest that, once a behavior has become a habit, environmental triggers are much more powerful than the promise of a reward. This is why it's so difficult to stop habits even after they stop being rewarding. The reward, or the motivational cue, may have been the thing that prompted you to first start the behavior, but once it becomes a habit, the signal that starts the habit loop in your brain is almost always environmental (Chen et al., 2020).

For example, when you're driving in the car, do you consciously think about putting your foot on the break when you see a red light? Or does it happen automatically? When you were first learning to drive, you probably did have to make the conscious decision to put your foot on the brake pedal. But now, all you have to do is see a red light or a stop sign for the habit loop of slowing down to be initiated. When you were first learning, you were motivated by reward (not crashing your car). Now that the behavior has become ingrained, the trigger has nothing to do with crashing the car. It's become an automatic response to an environmental trigger (the red light).

There are "red lights" all around us, triggering

habit responses without our awareness. You might start to get hungry at noon because you're hungry — or because you hear the music coming from the food truck where you typically buy lunch. The habit response of eating lunch isn't triggered by an inherent need to eat, but by a sound that your brain now associates with eating food. This is the reason that sleep experts often recommend not doing anything but sleep in your bed. If your bed is only for sleeping, then your brain will start to associate being asleep with being in your bed. The simple act of lying down will make you start to feel tired. But if you watch TV, read, scroll through your phone, and eat in bed, then your brain won't form an association between bed and sleep. Worse, it may develop an association between bed and one of these other activities. Whenever you get into bed, instead of your brain preparing to sleep, it may automatically become excited, ready to watch TV or go on social media.

A 2012 study demonstrated the power of context cues in triggering automatic habit responses (Wood, 2017). The study divided participants into people with a strong habit of running every day, those who were sporadic runners, and those who didn't run at all. First, participants cited the places where they typically ran (or would run, in the case of the nonrunners). Researchers asked the participants to visualize the place they had nominated as their typical running spot. Then, they asked them to read a short article and circle the words "running" and "jogging" every time they appeared in the text. The study found that habitual runners were much better able to find the words than sporadic or nonrunners. However, it also found that their ability to find those words dramatically decreased if they weren't asked to visualize their typical running locations first. What this study demonstrated was that simply visualizing their running route made them ready to run, to the point that they were more sensitive even to the word "running." The place and the activity prompt similar cognitive responses in the brain. Those who hadn't yet developed a running habit, on the other hand, had not yet formed these associative connections with their designated running routes.

The Routine

Think of the routine as the habit itself. This is the behavior that automatically plays when we are exposed to a certain environmental cue. Once you've done something enough, you'll find yourself automatically prompted to think, feel, or behave in a certain way in similar circumstances without any specific purpose or expectation of results. This is why you automatically lower your voice when you enter a library or start thinking more about your distant relatives in the weeks after Halloween. Your brain automatically associates the library with the lowering of your voice, and associates Thanksgiving with contacting your distant relatives. The circumstances are the "play" button on the behaviors, attitudes, or feelings that you've come to associate with that kind of situation.

When you start paying attention to your own habits, start trying to see the entire loop, from beginning to end. When you find yourself craving a cigarette or dreaming of the chocolate that you aren't supposed to have, pay attention to the environment around you. What do you think triggered that response? Is the place? The people you're with? The time of day? Are you on your way somewhere? Did you just get home from somewhere else? The better you are at identifying the environmental cues, the more aware you'll become of your own habit loops.

On the flip side, you can also use the power of context cues to form your own habit loops. If you always do your homework in the library, then soon you'll find that even walking toward the library gets you in the right mindset to study. If you always time your run to coincide with the sunrise, then you might find early morning light or the song of the birds at a certain time of the morning get you energized and wanting to go outside. Ironically, the routine is at the center of the habit loop, but it's the part of the loop that you have the least amount of control over. The more deeply associated the behavior is with a certain cue, the more automatic the routine becomes (Chen et al., 2020).

The more often you do, think, or say something in

a certain environment, the more automatic it becomes for you to do, think, or say that thing the next time you find yourself in that environment. The more automatic a behavior becomes, the more comfortable it feels. Speaking loudly in a church, for example, is probably something you'd have to consciously try to do, and it would probably feel strange or inappropriate. Even if the church was completely empty, it would feel strange to speak loudly because that kind of behavior would run contrary to your habit loop. You've developed a context association between whispers and church, and so doing anything else will feel very uncomfortable.

Routine behaviors are quite literally etched into our neural pathways. Over time, our brain forms certain connections in response to external or environmental information. Repetition is what creates these pathways, and it takes repetition in order to form new ones. The first time you act in a way that's contrary to your habit loop, your brain is in unfamiliar territory. By changing your environment or changing your behavior in a familiar environment, you are forcing your brain to make new connections. This is why starting a new habit or letting go of a bad habit can be so uncomfortable at first, even if the new habit is beneficial or provides you with some kind of reward. It's not enough to have one good night of sleep or one day feeling refreshed and energized. You have to repeat the new behavior over and over and create new environmental associations before it starts to feel comfortable.

Psychologists can divide all human behaviors into two loose categories: goal-directed and habitual (Chen et al., 2020). Goal-directed actions are the conscious choices that we make every single day. These are the ways in which we respond to new situations and new information, and they are largely regulated by their consequences. When faced with a new situation, we will naturally take the course of action we think is most likely to benefit us in that moment.

But habitual behaviors are reflexive. They are performed, not with the expectation of a certain outcome, but as a reaction to a specific situational trigger. Though most habits begin as goal-directed behaviors, the more automatic they become, the less of an influence the outcome has over whether or not the behavior is executed. This is why you find yourself eating that extra cookie or staying up just a few more hours even though you *know* it's bad for you. It's why you can't resist going out with your friends even though you have to wake up early the next morning, or how you find yourself putting off your work projects when your best friend calls you. If you're in the habit of chatting with your best friend every afternoon, then the rewards of picking up or ignoring the call have very little impact on whether or not you actually answer. Of course you want to talk to your friend, but the phone will be at your ear before you've even had time to think that thought. Where we often struggle to make or break habits, however, is overestimating the power and presence of the reward in the habit loop.

Perhaps not surprisingly, the simpler an activity is, the more easily it becomes a habit. A 2010 study found that it took as little as 18 days of repetition for simple tasks like riding a bicycle or drinking more water to become habitual, while it took an average of 254 days of consistent repetition before tasks like going to the gym became habitual (Duhigg, 2014). The reason for this, once again, has to do more with the environment than with the reward. Simple, or "recurrent" tasks, are performed almost the same way regardless of changing environmental conditions. The way you drink water on a hike, in a classroom, and in your office is basically identical, especially if you carry a water bottle with you. Your ability to successfully repeat the action of drinking water throughout the day is extremely high.

On the other hand, complex or "nonrecurrent" tasks require modifications in order to be successfully carried out, depending on external circumstances. If you're trying to get in the habit of going to the gym every day after work, all it takes is one day of having to stay late or one afternoon of being invited to go out with your coworkers to disrupt your ability to repeat the task. The more your ability to repeat the task is disrupted, the longer it takes for that action to become habitual. It doesn't matter how badly you want to go to the gym. Until your brain can form sufficient contextual associations, you'll have to consciously remind yourself to go to the gym.

The Reward

The reward is the final piece of the habit loop, and as such, it has a unique place in the loop. Once a behavior becomes a habit, the reward has a negligible effect on whether or not we perform that behavior. But in order for a behavior to be repeated enough to become a habit in the first place, there has to be some kind of reward. At the very least, the behavior has to help us avoid some kind of punishment or negative consequences.

Habit loops don't just form around repetition—they form around successful and satisfying repetition. Completing the action feels good, and so we do it again. Over time, our brain determines that X behavior is the best and most appropriate response to Y situation. Once the behavior becomes automatic, your brain doesn't need the promise of reward to execute the behavior anymore—the reward is assumed. Even if the reward changes or goes away altogether, the behavior is so ingrained that, in order to be successfully overcome, it must be replaced by a new habit that achieves a new reward.

Though identifying the cue is a critical part of habit formation, identifying the reward is equally as important. Arguably, the trigger and the reward are two sides of the same coin. For example, imagine that the habit you are trying to break is biting your nails. No matter what you try, you can't seem to stop. You've coated your fingernails in lemon juice, tried wearing gloves, and started painting your nails, all to no avail. But the essential flaw in all of these approaches is that they don't address the underlying reward, the one that caused you to develop the habit in the first place. Presumably, you didn't start biting your nails because they taste good or because you like the way your nails look after you've bitten them. To break this habit, you have to take a step back and identify the habit loop that it's part of. Why did you start biting your nails in the first place? What was the reward that caused you to repeat this behavior?

For many people, nail-biting is a stress response. Feelings of stress are the cue or the environmental trigger, and stress relief is the reward, so your habit loop will look something like this: stress — nail-biting — stress relief. At this point, nail-biting may no longer relieve your stress, but the behavior has become automatic. In order to stop or transform your behavior, you have to replace it with a new behavior that will provide you the same reward. Wearing gloves and dipping your fingers in lemon juice, presumably, are not great stress relievers. When you find yourself in stressful situations or when you find yourself feeling the urge to bite your nails, do something that relaxes you. Replace your nail-biting with deep breathing or a mindfulness exercise. Form a new habit loop, one that cues beneficial behaviors in times of stress, ones that do fulfill the reward of relieving that stress.

The rewards we get (or once got) from habitual behaviors aren't always obvious. Fulfillment, distraction, socializing, escapism, self-punishment, and simple excitement are all potential rewards at the end of our habit loops. In one way or another, our habits begin as coping mechanisms, ways that we have learned to navigate certain situations to our benefit. Once you've identified the environmental cues that prompt your habitual actions, the next question to ask yourself is how the habit itself made it easier for you to navigate that environment. For example, perhaps you always feel the urge to smoke cigarettes when you're feeling anxious. What about smoking cures your anxiety? Is it simply a distraction, something else to think about when you are feeling nervous? Perhaps you got in the habit of talking about your worries with friends while standing outside together smoking a cigarette. Years later, your life is changed and your friends are no longer there, but the action of smoking is now part of a habit loop that once led to the reward of much needed socialization. The behavior that you use to replace smoking will only be effective if it forms a similar bridge between the environment and the reward.

Achieving a certain reward is almost always the instigation that leads to the formation of new habits. When we are consciously trying to learn new behaviors, however, our goals and the rewards at the end of our habit loops don't always line up. For example, if you want to get yourself into the habit of eating healthy food, the reward that you are consciously hoping to achieve is probably something like improving your physical or cognitive wellness. But rewards that you gain from eating junk food are not necessarily going to be satisfied by your new meal plan. Furthermore, the rewards that you gain from eating junk food may not be what you think they are. Sure, you may have started eating junk food because it tastes good, but you might have started eating junk food at a low point in your life. Maybe foods like ice cream or mac n' cheese or hamburgers made you feel better because you associate them with childhood or summer picnics or other times in your life when you felt happy and loved. The reward from eating junk food, then, has less to do with taste and more to do with emotional comfort. Your new diet won't yield that reward because you don't have those same associations. To truly transform your junk food habit, then you'll have to find new behaviors that can yield the same reward in similar situations.

When we identify habits as "bad," it's typically because there's some way in which that habit is detrimental to our lives. But even "bad" habits are rewarding us in one way or another. Compulsive shopping might make you feel bad in the sense that it depletes your finances, clutters your home, and makes you feel guilty about spending money in frivolous ways. But chances are, it's continuing to satisfy the reward that it was initially built to achieve, and that alone is enough to make it feel safe, familiar, and satisfying. Identifying the environmental cues that cause you to start shopping online will often help you to identify the reward that shopping brings you. The next time you're in a similar situation, try initiating a different behavior that achieves the same reward.

3

Why Willpower Won't Work

When habits become automatic, they're… well, automatic. Since you don't consciously decide to perform them, consciously deciding *not* to perform them isn't enough to change your behavior — at least, not in the long term. The neurological patterns in the brain that are formed by habits are actually visible to scientists. Once the pathways have been established, you can't simply remove them. To truly transform habitual behavior, those pathways need to be rerouted. The same triggers and rewards need to be connected through different response mechanisms.

In fact, automaticity is such a powerful component of habit that this is how scientists distinguish habitual from goal oriented behavior. If you are able to halt or modify a behavior because you don't like the outcome, or because the outcome wasn't what you were expecting, then from a cognitive science perspective, this behavior cannot be considered a habit. Habits are behaviors that we repeat continuously and compulsively *regardless* of the outcome. The diminished power of the reward in habitual behavior is called "outcome insensitivity." Even if the initial reward has been satisfied, or is no longer being satisfied by the habitual behavior, the right triggers will engage the habitual response anyway (Wood, 2017).

However, though most cognitive scientists and behavioral psychologists agree that willpower alone isn't enough to overcome habitual behaviors, there is some disagreement as to the role willpower (our ability to self-regulate or control ourselves) plays in habit transformation. While some say that willpower has almost nothing to do with it, other behavioral psychologists insist that some degree of willpower is necessary in order to motivate you to want to change your behavior in the first place. Some have even suggested that the ability to transform habitual behavior is correlated with self-esteem. The higher your self-esteem, the better your ability to change habitual behaviors. The lower your self-esteem, the more vulnerable you are to destructive habits.

Though these kinds of psychological speculations can't be proven through neurological studies, one thing is clear — willpower alone is not enough, and for two major reasons (Wood, 2017). First, trying to combat habits with willpower underestimates their automaticity. It doesn't matter how badly you want to stop biting your nails or jog every morning. When exposed to your environmental cues, you're likely going to engage in the habitual behavior without even realizing what you're doing. Second, willpower is emotionally draining. The human brain responds much more powerfully to the promise of immediate, sensory pleasure than it does any other kind of stimulation, including avoidance of punishment or the ability to meet long-term goals. As such, simply saying "no" to yourself multiple times a day won't be enough to curb your habit. Eventually, your willpower will burn out, and you'll be right back where you started. This is why replacing or transforming habits is far more effective than simply trying to break them.

Rather than simply stopping or starting habits, this book will be focused on changing them. To do that, you do need a certain *amount* of willpower. Willpower is what motivates you to change in the first place. Willpower will be what inspires you to replace one behavior with another. It's what will prompt you to look more closely at your own behaviors, and what will help you to identify habit loops to help you build new connections between your cues and rewards.

When paired with the right approach to habit transformation, willpower can be a powerful source of motivation and energy. Willpower is what will keep you focused and on track when it comes to actively taking steps to change your life for the better. But willpower isn't the mechanism for change. When it comes to habit transformation, willpower is only effective when paired with clear goals and a designated replacement behavior.

When looking at habit transformation, behavioral psychologist Mark Manson insists that focusing on willpower means putting too much emphasis on the ultimate goal. The way we determine whether or not habits are "good" or "bad" is by looking at them in relation to our bigger life goals. We decide that drinking every night or eating cookies before dinner are "bad" habits because we want to lose weight or we want to be healthy. But the promise of losing weight in the future isn't enough to disrupt the habit loops that you've formed around eating or exercise or any other part of your life that you've determined is getting in the way of you achieving your goals. Willpower is the compass that gives you direction. It's what helps you to determine which habits need to change and to what end. Willpower is your GPS system, but simply plugging in the route isn't enough to physically get you to your destination. To do that, you have to break your habits down into their tiny loops. You have to determine what situations are triggering your bad habits, determine what routines or behaviors you want to replace them with, and how those new routines or behaviors are going to achieve the same rewards that you gained from the old habits.

From a neurological perspective, willpower has

nothing to do with habit transformation. Willpower exists in a part of your brain called the prefrontal cortex. This is the part of your brain that regulates conscious thinking, problem solving, and decision making. Goal inspired behaviors are initiated in the prefrontal cortex. Once those behaviors become habits, that part of the brain no longer lights up. Habitual pathways are formed in different parts of the brain, areas that control the ways we respond to environmental and emotional triggers. From a neurological standpoint, willpower and habits are apples and oranges. From a psychological standpoint, willpower can be a powerful motivator. It's the fuel in your tank, the thing that makes you want to attempt such a difficult undertaking as rerouting your brain. Without willpower, you're unlikely to make much progress when it comes to habit transformation. Willpower is only one small piece of the puzzle.

The Research

In 2009, a study was conducted to measure just how powerful the phenomenon of outcome insensitivity actually is (Duhigg, 2014). Participants in the study were shown a series of images. They were told that responding to one image would give them candy, while the other would earn them potato chips. After a few hours of routinely indicating their preferences in response to these images, participants were rewarded with their chosen snack, given as much as they could eat until they were fully satisfied. When tested again, the participants made almost 100% of the same image choices, even after reporting that they no longer needed or wanted the snack they had previously chosen. Their responses to the designated pictures had already become automatic, regardless of the proven outcome (Duhigg, 2014).

Not only does this study demonstrate how powerful outcome insensitivity is, but it demonstrates how quickly a simple action can become ingrained as a habit. The simpler the action, and the more immediate the reward, the faster the habitual pathways are built in the brain. This is why inspiring yourself with goals, attitudes, or concepts aren't as effective as we often want them to be. For example, your life goal might be to be a famous writer, and yet you find yourself spending far more time watching Netflix than working on your novel. This doesn't mean that you don't have what it takes to become a great writer. It just means that simply knowing what you want isn't enough. Becoming a great novelist is a wonderful goal, but there are hundreds of different ways that you could achieve that goal. The reward of publishing a great novel is one that exists in the long-term. Habits, on the other hand, don't respond to the long-term. They exist in the realm of the immediate, the sensory, and the familiar. If you've spent the past few months watching Netflix from 8pm to 2am every night, then when 8pm rolls around, you're going to find it very difficult to concentrate on anything else.

Even strongly desired goals are characterized by what psychologists call "equifinality." This means that they can be achieved through a number of different behavioral routes. The more behavioral options you have in front of you, the less likely you are to build up a repetitive pattern of behavior. Goals are big. They're complex. And most importantly, they're intentional. Habits, on the other hand, aren't intentional. They're automatic. They're the result of conditioning, not motivation. A change in motivation might mean a change in goals, but it doesn't necessarily mean a change in behaviors.

In fact, there's a great deal of research to suggest that associating self-control with habit performance can actually make you less likely to initiate meaningful change in your life. If you believe that habit transformation is all about willpower, then you will associate habit performance with failure or weakness. Every time you engage in the old habit, you will view this as a reflection on your powers of motivation or self-discipline. The inevitable discouragement that follows every lapse into the old habit will eventually stop you from trying to change, or worse, cause you to initiate new behaviors that are meant to "punish" yourself. Self-punishing behaviors can take an even more severe psychological toll than bad habits, and when taken to an extreme, can be physically destructive as well.

Control of habits and unwanted behavior responses is something that humans have been studying for centuries (Sims, 2018). Behavior control was once the territory of state religions, but in our modern age, it's becoming more and more the realm of scientists and psychologists. Over the years, a number of different strategies have been proposed to help the average person to cope with unwanted behaviors, thoughts, or feelings. But at the end of the day, the most pervasive and effective self-control strategies have not relied on desire alone. From the power of prayer to the 12-step AA method, behavior control strategies merely begin with the desire to change. But all effective habit transformation strategies or programs offer a routine to replace the unwanted habit.

A 2010 study examined the efficacy of different strategies that people use to overcome unwanted behaviors or emotional impulses throughout their lives (Wood & Rünger, 2016). About 12% of the unwanted impulses reported by participants in the study were considered "strongly habitual," meaning that they were behaviors performed almost every day in similar contexts. 38% of the unwanted stimuli, however, were triggered by emotional situations (Wood & Rünger, 2016). These behaviors may not have been performed daily, but they were performed automatically in response to certain emotional triggers like stress, depression, or even sexual arousal. Though all of these behaviors could be considered habits in the sense that they were performed automatically in response to a specific circumstance, coping strategies that worked for the more routine, situationally triggered habits didn't necessarily work for the emotionally triggered habits, and vice versa.

This is why understanding habit loops is so vital for effective habit change. Understanding the trigger and the initial reward makes a critical difference in the approach you might take in tackling that habit. A habit triggered by feelings of insecurity is not going to be managed the same way as a habit triggered by time of day. Perhaps more importantly, habits with emotional triggers lead to very different kinds of rewards than routine habits that come from intentional repetition. Tying your left shoe first, for example, may not have any kind of reward at all. It's just that you are left handed, so you happened to go for the left foot the very first time you ever tied a shoe, and since nothing bad happened to prevent you from starting with the left shoe, it never occurred to you to change things up. If you wanted to change this habit, the mechanisms you would use would be very different from the mechanisms you would use to change your habit of drinking on Saturday mornings, which began as a college tradition that you started with your friends, that then became a habit with the situational trigger of Saturday mornings and the previous reward fulfillment of social time with friends.

The Myth of Self-Control

Self-control is what happens when we consciously make the decision not to do something that we really want to do. Self-control is how you make yourself leave the New Years' Eve Party at 11:00pm because you have a big project due January 2nd and you need to spend the next day working. Self-control is how you decide to do your homework before you watch TV, and how you decide not to drink when you're on call with the hospital. Self-control exists in the prefrontal cortex, and has a great deal of influence when it comes to the ways we encounter new situations or handle life's challenges. Self-control, however, has almost nothing to do with habits.

More specifically, self-control is more effective in curbing habits that are triggered by routine situations. If you want to wake up an hour earlier, for example, you simply set your alarm to the appropriate time. When it rings, you fill your mind with positive images of the amazing new job that you just got and drag yourself out of bed. Do this enough times, and you have a new habit. Sounds easy, yes?

This kind of thinking doesn't quite work with habits that are emotionally triggered. The trouble comes when we don't know if our triggers are situational (time of day, physical environment, weather) or emotional (stress, depression, sensory pleasure). If it's natural for you to wake up at 7am because that's simply what you've always done, then forcing yourself to wake up at 6am might actually be possible.

But imagine that you absolutely can't stand your job. You hate your boss, you don't get along with your colleagues, you're overworked and most definitely underpaid. Hitting the snooze button, in this situation, might not be a matter of willpower after all. You are in the habit of sleeping until 7am because you don't want to go to work, not because you're not used to waking up at 6am. In this situation, the trigger that causes you to hit the snooze button isn't motivated by routine, it's triggered by feelings of dread before going to work.

Now imagine that you get a new job. You love this job. It's everything you've ever wanted. The working environment is great, you get along with your colleagues, and it's in a field that you're passionate about. But you still find yourself unable to get out of bed on time. Why? Because your brain has built a context association between your alarm ringing and going to a horrible job that you hate. Before you even realize what you've done, you've hit the snooze button and gone back to sleep. Willpower might make you aware of your bad habit, but in this case, it's not going to be enough to change your habit.

Many studies have found that the most effective way is to change or avoid the trigger that initiates unwanted habit loops (Wood, 2017). This is much easier said than done. Most habits are created unintentionally, and therefore, it isn't always obvious what the trigger is or even what the initial reward was. A 2010 study found that careful self-monitoring was actually more effective than trigger avoidance, simply because many participants didn't fully understand what their triggers were (Manson, 2019). However, the study found that this intense self-monitoring was only marginally more successful at changing the unwanted habits.

Self-control (what the study called "vigilant monitoring") is far more effective at making us aware of our automatic impulses and behaviors, but it's not a great tool for actually correcting the unwanted behavior. It's nearly impossible to change habits without some level of self-control, but self-control is just the first step (Manson, 2019).

Many studies have also found that self-control is a lot more complicated than it seems. Factors like distraction, cognitive decline related to age, time pressure, and even limited task ability can all eat away at an individual's self-control. So even if stress isn't a trigger for your bad habits, you'll find yourself much less able to control your behavior when you're feeling tired, distracted, or otherwise cognitively impaired than when you're relaxed and focused. Since it's inevitable that you aren't going to feel relaxed and focused 100% of the time, it's almost guaranteed that a situational lapse in cognitive ability will disrupt your self-discipline when it comes to controlling or suppressing an unwanted habit.

Making the decision to act differently than usual

in a familiar situation requires willpower. But when your willpower resources have been drained or compromised by other cognitive demands, you inevitably fall back on your habitual behaviors to see you through the situation at hand. To illustrate the point, a 2005 study looked at participants who had formed the habit of keeping their personal feelings to themselves. All of the participants in the study were actively trying to increase their ability to disclose personal thoughts or feelings (Wood, 2017). When relaxed and focused, participants showed a marked ability to change their habitual responses. However, when the same participants were asked to perform a difficult task before entering a social situation, they were far more likely to fall back on their old habits, even when personal disclosure was the socially appropriate response. Feelings of tiredness or distraction were enough to exhaust their self-control, preventing them from making lasting change to their social behaviors.

The way to truly initiate lasting, behavioral change is to create new habits, ones that neurologically compete with the old ones. Self-control is what will inspire you to do this, but it's not enough to actually rewire the pathways in your brain. Deep, lasting habit transformation means creating automaticity around beneficial behaviors. Rather than consciously trying to share your feelings, for example, effective change would mean finding alternative behaviors that give you the same sense of security that emotional withdrawal provided you in social situations. Self-control is often the thing that makes you aware of your automatic responses. In the beginning, simple self-control might be the thing that illuminates what your real triggers or rewards are, but self-control alone is not enough to make, break, or transform your habits.

4

The Importance of a Goal

Before you start exerting your willpower over your behaviors, you need to have a strong goal in place. Goals tell you why you want to change your habits in the first place. More importantly, they give you guidance as to how you want to transform your habits. You'll find yourself with a lot more motivation if you have a clear understanding as to why you're trying to change and what you're hoping to gain from modifying your behaviors and routines.

To truly change your behavior, there needs to be a strong enough reason. Your goal for changing your behavior acts as a kind of internal compass, a guide for you to follow when things get difficult. Willpower alone is useless if it's applied out of context. If you want to go to bed earlier or eat better, you have to have a good reason for it. The vague, often societally based reasons like "being healthy" are often not good

Creating New Habits

enough to keep you committed. Why exactly do you want to change your habits? What about your habit is "bad"? Which of your life goals is your habit stopping you from achieving? What hardships is your habit causing that could be avoided if you transformed that habit into something more beneficial?

Unfortunately, the realization that our habits have turned bad comes at a point that Alcoholics Anonymous terms "rock bottom." This typically takes the form of a major life event, something drastic and negative that was directly instigated by the negative habit in question. While it's possible to change your habits before hitting rock bottom, we often don't believe that we have a problem until something dramatic happens. Habits are small, sometimes miniscule. As such, it's easy to convince ourselves that they don't have a major influence over the quality of our lives, and that we could change our behavior at any time, if only we wanted to. It's unpleasant to think of ourselves as organic robots, playing behavior tapes in response to certain environmental stimuli. We want to believe that we are fully in control of our actions, and so we often convince ourselves we aren't changing our behavior because it "isn't a big deal" or it's not the "real" problem. It's only when we hit rock bottom that we have no choice but to see ourselves for who we really are, and recognize that there's more governing our behaviors than active, conscious decision-making.

The most effective goals are specific. They directly

answer the question "Why do I want to stop/change this habit?" As an example, let's look at the story of Lisa (Duhigg, 2014). She had a number of problematic, compulsive behaviors. She was addicted to both smoking and drinking. She was a compulsive spender, had difficulty regulating her anger, and found herself with more than $20,000 in delinquent credit debt before the age of 30. By the age of 40, she had completely turned her life around. Not only had she managed to quit smoking, drinking, and shopping, but she had a successful professional life, a healthy credit score, and was in better physical shape than she had been when she was 25. How did she do it?

While it's easy to believe that Lisa just had an iron will (and certainly, willpower came into play throughout her journey), there's a lot more to her story than that. The thing that really motivated her to change her life came in the form of a dramatic event. She, like so many others, had to hit rock bottom before she was able to admit that her habits were both destructive and out of her control. Her rock bottom came in the form of a divorce from her husband, after which he and his new girlfriend traveled to Cairo. Lisa followed them there, thinking of getting revenge on her husband for leaving her. After a dramatic altercation, during which her ex-husband made it clear they were never getting back together, she decided to take a trip across the Egyptian desert. She wasn't sure if this trip was even possible, but one thing believed was certain—in order to make that trip, she would have to quit smoking.

Lisa's decision to quit smoking was directly linked to the achievement of a specific goal—making the trip across the desert. It was this "why," this goal, that motivated her to replace smoking with the more beneficial habit of jogging. And while it might seem impossible that quitting smoking would help her to completely turn her life around, changing that one habit created a cascade effect in her life. As it turned out, many of the triggers that instigated her other bad habits were related to the triggers that caused her to smoke. In fact, some habits (like drinking), were triggered by the act of smoking itself! Though bigger, vaguer life goals like being healthier are certainly worth pursuing, they aren't great motivators for habit change because they're too big, and too vague. But the small, specific goal of making the trip across the Egyptian desert was perfect, and enough for Lisa to not only quit smoking, but transform her life entirely.

Habits are very small, specific actions that are only triggered by certain situations. As such, they don't respond well to big, long-term goals because it's too easy to fit that habit into vague, big picture schemes. You may be determined to quit smoking in order to "live healthier," but it's too easy to achieve that same goal by eating healthy or doing yoga every morning. More importantly, being "healthy" isn't a concrete reward, something that you can work toward and definitely achieve. Again, this doesn't mean it's not a worthy goal, but as far as habits are concerned, the rewards aren't concrete enough to give you sufficient determination to change. A goal like Lisa's, on the other hand, was both small and specific. The trip was her reward for quitting smoking, and the promise of the trip gave her enough determination to commit to transforming her habit even when it was difficult. It had her a specific timeline, which meant there was no room for her to slide back into her old habits. Every day that she lit up a cigarette instead of going for a jog pushed her dream of going on her trip back further.

How to Set Goals

When setting goals, it's very important to remain true to what you want, and not what you think is possible. Because the majority of our habits go unnoticed, we have a tendency to subconsciously set goals that are based on our habits. But to be truly successful in achieving the lives that we want, we have to take the opposite approach. Setting good goals enables you to create habits based on your goals.

In many cases, the erosion of willpower when it comes to transforming habits has to do with a subconscious shift in goals. The more you drink or stay out partying on the weekends, the harder it is to picture yourself following your dream of becoming a surgeon. Slowly, over time, you convince yourself that surgery just "isn't for you," and your ability to self-regulate unwanted habits becomes more and more limited as your goals seem more and more unattainable.

This is why the simple act of writing down your goal can be so powerful. Rather than allowing your habits to influence what you "can" and "can't" do, writing your goals down gives you a physical reminder of what you want to achieve. It also reminds you that you *can* achieve that goal, and that transforming your habit is simply the first step in your long-term plan. Keeping your eye on an ultimate prize that you really want will provide you with all the motivation you need to transform even the most deeply ingrained habits.

Furthermore, setting specific goals will help you to determine how you want to transform your habits. For example, if your goal is to become a great writer, you may want to replace your drinking with writing, or your partying with open mic nights. If your goal is to become a surgeon, you might want to replace your drinking with jogging, or your partying with studying. Setting specific goals will help you to determine which habits are "bad" in the first place. Any habit that's holding you back from achieving what you want should be transformed into something that will get you closer to your goals or maintaining the lifestyle that you want (Wood, 2017).

People who aren't aware of their habit loops will

have to guess at the reasons why they've developed a certain habitual behavior. If you're aware of the behavior, but you aren't aware of the cue, then you only have a limited ability to reflect on how the behavior got started in the first place. Worse, many people tend to assume that if a behavior is repeated and often and difficult to let go of, then it must align somehow with their "true" needs or goals. Studies have shown that people assume habits are favorable based on how difficult alternative behaviors are. For example, one study of consumer behavior demonstrated that people were more likely to continue using the same products or services out of habit (Dean, 2013). But when asked why they were resistant to using new products or skills, almost all participants insisted that the new (unfamiliar) products were somehow inferior. An objective study of the two products or services, however, proved this assumption false. This study demonstrated just how difficult it can be to recognize habitual behaviors for what they are, and how easy it is to make assumptions about ourselves, others, and the world around us based on what feels comfortable. We all think we're immune to this kind of thinking, but how often have you thought to yourself something like, "Well, if I *really* wanted to be in a band it wouldn't be so difficult for me to practice my guitar" or "I really should study for this exam, but it's also important for me to have good relationships with my friends. I can skip this one night…"

These rationalizations underplay the automaticity

of habitual behaviors. In fact, many psychological studies have shown that the presence of persistent bad habits has nothing to do with the ability to set strong goals or intentions. And as we know, the promise of reward or the desire for a certain outcome no longer has any influence on a behavior that's become a habit. Habits are persistent and hard to transform simply because they're automatic. If a habit is particularly difficult to break, that doesn't necessarily reflect some kind of internal conflict or reveal anything about your motivation to achieve your goals. Don't set goals based on your habits. Transform habits to help you achieve your goals (Duhigg, 2014).

Sometimes habitual behaviors or compulsions are so strong that people invent internal motivations to explain their persistent inability to change (Wood, 2017). Addicts, especially, complain of the compulsive need to drink or use drugs. However, some psychological studies have suggested that this compulsion is not a precursor to using drugs, but rather a rationalization of their behavior that happens after the fact. Something similar happens in people who struggle with obsessive compulsive behaviors. Habits happen without any kind of conscious decision being made. In order to understand who we are and why we continue to act in this way, we retrospectively determine what must have been going through our minds when we engaged in the habitual behavior. The danger of this is that it can cause us to come to certain conclusions about who we are and how much control we actually have over our own lives.

Setting goals can help you to avoid drawing these kinds of conclusions. Your goals have much more to say about your personality, desires, and internal motivations than your habits. Rather than letting your compulsive behaviors define who you are, you can look toward your goal and let the pursuit of your dreams be the thing that determines your character. Good goal setting helps us to view habits for what they are—automatic programs that once served us, but that are no longer doing their job. Setting a goal will help you to not only see the habits that must be changed, but to see the loops that they are part of. Understanding your cues and rewards can help you to choose the most appropriate replacement routines, ones that will not only effectively transform your bad habit, but will get you closer to achieving your personal dreams and goals.

The Power of Intention

When habits follow our intentions, we find the switch from one habit to the other much easier. For example, imagine that you've decided to switch from eating white to whole grain bread. You buy it from the supermarket for a few weeks in a row. You find that you like it, especially with certain butters or spreads, and so you keep buying it. After a few months, you're automatically looking for whole grain bread, and

Creating New Habits

white bread is a distant memory. This is how habit transformation can work in your favor. You set the intention of eating better, you determine which habits are working against that intention, you choose a replacement behavior that will align with your intention when exposed to the same triggers, and you commit until the replacement routine has overridden the old one.

Using intention as a guide to help you transform your habits isn't just for physical actions, either. Mental and emotional habits benefit greatly from intention setting as well. For example, perhaps you've come to resent your romantic partner for being selfish. But a mutual friend insists that you're being too harsh, and provides you with multiple examples of times when your partner was quite giving and selfless. You determine to make more of an effort to recognize selfless behavior in your partner. You make a mental note every time they buy you a drink or are there to listen to your problems. Before you know it, your mental habit of labeling your partner as selfish has been transformed.

Intentions are like a guiding star for our behaviors. They show us what we want to change and how we can change them. The reason for this is because intentions enable us to spot patterns, and our brains love patterns. As a species, humans are extremely good at pattern recognition. We are wired to enjoy repetition to a certain degree, and that enjoyment of repetition can be used to quickly and easily transform bad habits into more beneficial ones if we have an intention to guide us.

An example of how powerful pattern recognition can be in our brains comes from a classic psychological study. Participants sat in front of individual computers for a total of four hours. They were asked to press one of four buttons, depending on where the image of a cross appeared on their screens. What the participants were not told was that there was a pattern to how the cross appeared on the screen. The pattern wasn't consciously recognizable, but over the course of the four hours, participants began responding faster and faster to the cross's movement on the screen. Through blind repetition, the participants had learned the pattern without even realizing that there was a pattern to learn.

This is essentially how habits form in our brains. We encounter the same situation over and over again, and respond in the way that is most favorable to us at the time. If we gain the same reward from the same behavior enough times, then that behavior becomes a habit. We've learned the pattern, the habit loop, without even realizing it. Typically, it's only when the pattern is broken, when the habit loop no longer rewards us but actively incurs destruction, that we even notice the habit in the first place.

With intention, however, we make the conscious decision to learn (and unlearn) a certain mental or behavioral pattern. Unconscious pattern recognition can imprint all kinds of behaviors and attitudes in our minds. Setting intentions and goals is what protects from these random imprints and helps us to develop behaviors that are beneficial to us. It's only through intention that we can build up a series of small habits that help us to achieve more complex goals. Think about learning complex mathematics or a foreign language. When you first start, it's extremely difficult. You spend hours pouring over flash cards, trying to remember that "red" is "roja" or "hello" is "hola." But after enough repetition, the new words, phrases, and grammar come easier and easier. Once you've made these patterns habitual, you can then move on to learn more complex words and phrases.

Habit transformation is most powerful when we use big life goals to determine which behaviors we want to ingrain in our subconscious minds, and which need to be overwritten in favor of something new. Like learning the foreign language, setting goals can help you to develop beneficial behaviors that build off of one another. If your big life goal is to "be wealthy," for example, setting that intention can help you to break that goal down into small, daily behaviors that will enable you to both achieve that goal, and maintain it once you have it. Like starting with "hello" and "goodbye," your initial intentions are going to be small and basic, things like "save $5 a week" or "make coffee at home instead of buying it from Starbucks." Once these behaviors have become habitual, however, you can start to build off of them, eventually building a complex network of beneficial habits that all work together to help you achieve your lifelong goal of being wealthy.

Intentions typically flow directly into our habits. If we want something, we look for ways to get it. This impulse is so strong and so elemental that a number of psychological studies have demonstrated that intention is the number one predictor of future behavior. If you consciously decide that you want to be wealthy, you're more likely to save than someone who doesn't. However, it's important to consciously make decisions about what we want because if we don't, our brains will look for patterns anyway. Many of our habits (especially bad ones) start completely by accident. We just happen to be in a certain environment or around certain people and all of a sudden, we have all these behavioral programs that have nothing to do with our goals or intentions. In fact, these behaviors may even run contrary to our goals and inventions. But if we aren't aware of this fact, it's too easy to assume that those strong, habitual behaviors were created for a reason, and that the development of the habit has something to do with what we "truly" want or who we truly are.

When setting your own intentions, don't be afraid or ashamed to set goals that are true to who you are. For example, if you want to quit smoking but the ultimate goal of "being healthy" just isn't motivating you, look for reasons to quit that are true to your life. Maybe a more powerful intention would be to create a healthy home environment for your children, or because cigarettes are expensive and you want to save money. Don't let society determine your intentions for you. Remain true to yourself, true to your goals. You'll find your habits much easier to transform when they start to align with the things that you really want for yourself, rather than the things you think you should want for yourself.

5

Changing Your Habits

Habit loops can't be removed. Once your brain builds the neural connections, they can't be dismantled. They can, however, be replaced. Think of your neural pathways like a set of wires. You can't throw them away and start from scratch, but you can move them around to form new connections. Simply quitting is rarely enough. To effectively break a bad habit, you have to choose a new behavior, something beneficial that will replace the old habit.

This chapter will provide you with a practical, 3-Step process toward habit transformation. No matter how deeply ingrained your bad habit is or what you wish to replace it with, this process can work for you. However, while the process is simple, it's rarely easy. Habit transformation is difficult. It will take time for the replacement behavior to feel comfortable and natural. If you're battling a chemical addiction, you may experience some unpleasant physical side effects.

Creating New Habits

If the behavior you wish to change has an emotional trigger, you may have to try a few different replacement behaviors before you find one that provides the same emotional reward. But just remember that you can do it. The secret to habit formation is repetition. If you stick with it, you will be able to change, no matter how impossible it might feel at first.

Before you can set a strong goal or engage the 3-step process, however, you first have to identify the trigger. What environmental or emotional cue instigates the habit loop that you are trying to break? Determining the real cue can sometimes take time, especially with habits that have gone on for years. Be patient with yourself throughout this process. Be aware of your environment and your mental state whenever you find yourself engaging in the unwanted behavior. What tripped the loop? What was the "play" button that caused your brain to activate this particular program? It may be something obvious, but it may not. Many habits develop from an initial intention, but many habits also develop by accident. The things that cue your behaviors might surprise you. They might even seem like they have nothing to do with the behavior or the reward. Often, the things that cue negative behaviors are things that we don't want to admit have that much power over our lives. But identifying the true trigger is critical for successful habit transformation. If you don't know what's causing the habit loop, then you'll find yourself automatically engaging in the behavior without really understanding why. Identifying the trigger will help you to identify the true rewards that you once gained from the behavior, and this will help you to determine the most appropriate replacement behavior.

You don't need to go to an expensive, formal treatment program in order to stop a problematic behavior, no matter how serious or destructive it is. People successfully transform their lives on their own all the time. It's not always easy, but it's certainly possible. Sometimes the most difficult part is the honest self-reflection that's required at the beginning of the process. To truly transform your behavior, you'll have to take an honest look at the cues, cravings, and rewards that trigger and motivate your problematic behaviors, and then find a way to replace your destructive behaviors with beneficial ones.

The most important element of habit change, however, is this last part. Without a replacement routine, lasting change is almost impossible. The old habit loops will never disappear from your brain, no matter how strong your willpower is or how much you try to avoid the old triggers. You can't control the way that your brain works, and you can't control the world around you. No matter how determined you are to "quit," you'll inevitably find yourself exposed to the old cues, whether those cues are feelings like stress or boredom, or environmental cues like being in a certain room. The moment your brain gets the cue, it will engage the old behavior. The only way to break this process is to give your brain an alternative response, a different program to play in response to the same signal.

Studies of alcoholics have found that people who achieve permanent change are the people who find new routines that both draw on the old triggers and provide the same relief (Wood, 2017). When looking at their habit loops, they realized that they couldn't change the triggers, and that their brain would still crave the rewards that alcohol once gave them. To effectively, permanently stop drinking, they would have to replace their drinking habit with one that could be adequately inserted into the old habit loop. When determining to transform your own habits, the goal is not to break or erase your habit loops. You're simply taking out the middle routine and replacing it with something beneficial, something that will both provide the reward in response to the environmental trigger and help you to cultivate a lifestyle that's aligned with your long-term goals.

Just because you aren't engaging in a formal treatment plan, however, does not mean that you have to battle your destructive habits alone. In fact, multiple studies have demonstrated that your chances of successful transformation increase dramatically when you do so as part of a group (Wood, 2017). Believing that you can do it is necessary. If you give up hope or start to believe that your old habits are unbreakable, you'll lose the necessary motivation that you need to stay committed. Being part of a group or community can help you to hold onto belief in yourself and belief in success. Communities provide you with encouragement when you're feeling down, and examples of others who have successfully fought the same battles you're facing now. As much as possible, find other people or groups that you can engage to help you transform your habit. Find someone else, whether it's a friend, a coworker, or an online community, who is struggling with the same habit. No matter how strange or specific you think your habit is, there's almost certainly someone else out there struggling with the same behavior. They may have different cues or have been gaining different rewards, but if you find someone to transform with you, then you'll have the emotional benefit of someone cheering you on.

The 3-Step Process

This simple, 3-step process is a journey in self-discovery. Following these steps will help you to identify your habit loops. You will become aware of both your triggers and your rewards, which will then enable you to choose an appropriate and effective replacement behavior. Identifying habit loops can sometimes be trickier than it appears, and so following these steps may take some time and reflection. Be patient with yourself. For many people, following these steps often takes more time than actively changing their behaviors!

Step One: Awareness Training

The first step in transforming your habits is to observe yourself. It's during this step that you will really come to terms with your triggers and rewards. If you can, keep a journal where you can record your observations and start to find patterns. Remain as focused as possible on what's happening around you when the habit starts. Before you start biting your nails, do you feel a tingling or itching feeling in your fingers? Are you feeling stressed or anxious? Are you with a certain person or in a specific place? What is the time of day? The time of year? Is there a specific holiday coming up? Are you returning home from a specific event? Be as observant as possible of your surroundings. Record every detail of your environment, both externally and internally, every time you find yourself engaging in the problematic behavior. Eventually, you will start to notice a pattern. Those patterns will help you to discover your cues.

Be patient during this process, as it can take some thinking. For example, perhaps you're trying to break the habit of buying a coffee the moment you get to work. Presumably your office or workspace is the environmental cue, but is there anything else going on? Are you more likely to crave that morning coffee when you're stressed or when your commute was particularly difficult? Is there a certain person or social situation that you feel you're missing out on when you refrain from buying that coffee? If you make coffee at home before heading to work, do you still find yourself buying a coffee when you get to work? Do you crave a cup of coffee at the same time in the morning on the weekends or when you're on vacation? The cue might simply be physically being in your office, but it might not. More specifically, the rewards that you get from that cup of coffee may not be what you expect. If coffee is the way you wake up your brain in the morning, then making coffee at home might be enough to curb your craving. But it won't be enough to stop your brain from playing that program when you get to the office. In order to truly stop yourself from buying that coffee, you have to find a replacement routine, something else to occupy your time when you first get to work that will satisfy you just as much.

Step Two: Why Do You Do It?

Once you've determined the trigger, the next step is to determine the reward. This can sometimes be even more difficult than determining the trigger, so be patient with yourself. The rewards of our habitual behaviors aren't always obvious. If this is a habit you've been doing for years, the initial rewards may no longer apply or be relevant to your current situation. But determining the reward is a very important step, so be patient with yourself as you try to find the answer. The reward will tell you which kinds of replacement routines will be most appropriate. One

Creating New Habits

of the biggest obstacles to successful habit transformation is when people try to replace their old habits with new routines that would make sense for the situation, but that don't satisfy them in the same way that their old habits did. To truly make effective change, you have to find an alternative, beneficial way to give yourself the same rewards. To do that, you need to determine what those rewards are.

Rewards don't have to be concrete, either. Many habits are unintentionally created to satisfy elemental urges like stress relief, distraction from boredom, the desire to be social, or even feelings of hunger. Stress and boredom, in particular, are two mental states that are actually quite cognitively taxing. Many habits evolve to help our brains cope with these difficult mental states. The behaviors that it chooses to relieve these feelings, however, are often entirely random, and have more to do with the environment in which these behaviors formed than they do with the mental state itself.

For example, imagine that the habit you're trying to break is going to the cafeteria for a snack after just one hour of work. It happens like clockwork—you get to your desk at 9am, but by 10am you find yourself wandering into the cafeteria. You believe it's because you're really hungry in the morning. You may even experience feelings of hunger around this time. To curb this routine, you've tried bringing healthy snacks to work, eating a bigger breakfast, and even taking your lunch an hour earlier, all to no avail. The reason none of these strategies work, however, is because the reward you get from going to the cafeteria isn't hunger relief after all—it's boredom relief. The routine that you choose to replace your morning snack, paradoxically, must be something that relieves feelings of boredom in order to be truly effective, rather than satisfying feelings of hunger. Once you find a replacement routine that stimulates your interest, you will probably find that your feelings of morning hunger disappear.

Sometimes, in order to determine the true rewards behind our destructive habits, we need to try a few different replacement routines. In the example of the morning snack, you may want to start by attempting to replace your cafeteria walk with a healthy snack from home. But if this isn't satisfactory, and you find yourself abandoning your lunchbox day after day, then you may want to take a step back and reevaluate whether or not your chosen replacement routine is giving you the same rewards as your destructive habit.

Step Three: The Reward

Once you've determined the true rewards of your destructive behavior, you'll feel a moment of clarity. "After biting my nails, I feel emotionally fulfilled." "After drinking my morning coffee I'm ready and motivated to work." "After eating a chocolate bar, I feel like my dinner is complete." Once you really get to the true root of your destructive behaviors, choosing the appropriate replacement behavior will be simple, especially with a strong goal in place. Understanding why you want to change your behavior, and understanding what emotional or sensory rewards the behavior satisfies, will make the process of active change much easier and more effective.

Once you've completed the 3-step process, you'll be ready to select a replacement routine and begin taking actionable steps to make changes in your real life. You might find that the initial replacement routine that you've chosen doesn't quite work, but that's ok. If you have a clear understanding of the habit loop, both in terms of its cues and its rewards, then you'll be much more effective in choosing a replacement behavior that you can reasonably expect yourself to commit to. When choosing a replacement routine, remember that the simpler the behavior, the easier it will be to transform into a habit. The most effective way to transform destructive habits is to find a replacement routine that's less complex than the destructive habit. The easier it is to successfully complete your new behavior, the easier it will be to repeat it.

This 3-step process is ultimately designed to help you become aware of your habit loops. Only at that point can you create an action plan that you will actually be able to commit to. No matter how closely your replacement behavior fits into the old habit loop, remember that it will still feel uncomfortable at first.

Habits are things that we've done over and over again. This means that, no matter how destructive or unpleasant they've become overtime, they are also extremely familiar. Our brains are wired to like familiar. Doing something new and different might be fun, exciting, and fulfilling, but it can also feel very uncomfortable. No matter which routine you choose to replace your old behavior, give yourself enough time to give it a good try before you decide to modify or try something else. The first few times will always feel strange. That's part of the process (Duhigg, 2014).

If at all possible, try replacing destructive habits with things that you've always wanted to do, but didn't have the "time" to do. For example, imagine that you've always wanted to learn a foreign language. Whenever you find yourself reaching for a cigarette or the TV remote, reach for your phone instead. Use the time that you would spend taking "smoke breaks" or watching TV to study Spanish on a language learning app.

To illustrate how the 3-step process will help you to create an effective plan for habit transformation, let's look at a few examples.

Example #1: Biting Nails

You want to stop biting your nails because it contradicts your life goals of being healthy or attractive. You find yourself biting your nails in response to feelings of stress or insecurity, and after engaging in the behavior, you feel a sense of emotional satisfaction. To replace this behavior then, try a routine like chewing gum or deep breathing. These behaviors will bring your daily life more closely in alignment with your goals of living in a healthier way or having better hygiene. Unlike painting your nails or dipping them in lemon juice, however, these replacement routines are both proven to reduce feelings of stress and increase feelings of emotional security. As such, these replacements will be much easier for you to commit to because they will provide the same relief in moments of stress that the nail-biting once provided.

Example #2: Coffee Addiction

You want to stop drinking coffee in the morning because buying a coffee every day contradicts your financial goals, and it contradicts your dietary goals by making you chemically dependent on caffeine to properly wake up in the morning. After drinking coffee, you feel settled and ready to start your work. Even drinking coffee at home before you get to work won't fill the hole in your routine that your morning coffee satisfies. As a replacement routine, try drinking herbal tea or water instead of coffee in the morning. Even if you purchase a tea from the same shop, teas are often much cheaper than coffee drinks. Both of these drinks, then, will bring your daily routine more closely in alignment with your goals of saving money and not being caffeine dependent. They will also help you preserve your daily routine as closely as possible, especially if you purchase your tea from the same shop or drink water out of the same mug that you once drank your coffee from.

Example #3: Eating Chocolate After Dinner

You want to stop your destructive habit of eating chocolate after dinner because it contradicts your dietary goals of consuming less sugar and your goal of losing a certain amount of weight. No matter how big your meal, however, the consumption of chocolate has become a ritual for you. As such, you don't feel full until you've consumed your bar of chocolate. A possible replacement routine could be eating a bowl of sweet fruits like grapes or strawberries after dinner. Since sweet fruits contain no refined sugars, this routine will keep your daily habits in alignment with your goals of consuming less sugar and losing weight. The act of separately eating the fruit will replace the ritual of eating the chocolate, helping to satisfy you without increasing your dinner portions. And the sweetness of the fruit will help you to feel like you're still consuming a treat or dessert, making this routine much easier to commit to than replacing your chocolate bar with a salty treat like peanuts or potato chips.

6

Experiment with New Routines

At this point, you've completed the 3-step process and have successfully identified your loop. For example, your loop might look something like this: boredom—going to the cafeteria for a snack—distraction. Or like this: anxiety—biting nails—stress relief. Now it's time for you to create an action plan.

Of the three parts of your habit loop, the only part that will change is the middle, the problematic behavior. The goal is to replace this behavior with something productive and positive. The cue will remain the same, as it's something that you can't realistically expect yourself to control. And the reward must remain the same in order for the replacement behavior to be effective.

The nature of your cue and reward will determine which replacement behavior is most appropriate. To this end, you may have to experiment with a few different replacement behaviors before you find one that sticks. For example, nail biting is an extremely common habit that's typically cued by feelings of stress and anxiety. If these are also your cues, then you may find deep breathing or other mindfulness techniques to be an appropriate replacement behavior.

However, as in the case of Mary Sims, simple stress reduction techniques weren't enough to curb her nail-biting habit (Sims, 2018). Why? Because there was a second cue that caused her to specifically develop the stress management habit of nail-biting, and that was an oral fixation. The act of putting something in her mouth was a key reason why she had unconsciously developed this particular habit, rather than developing some other stress reducing habit. Deep breathing may achieve the same reward and be an appropriate response to the same trigger, but it didn't satisfy the oral fixation.

Once she realized this, Mary changed her tactic. Rather than trying to replace her nail-biting with deep breathing, she replaced it with chewing gum. This effectively addressed both the anxiety and the oral fixation that had caused her to develop her habit. Chewing gum has been found in many studies to reduce feelings of stress (Duhigg, 2014), and Mary was no exception. After years and years of trying various tactics to break her habit, chewing gum helped her to break her "unbreakable" habit within a matter of months.

Of course, that doesn't mean that it was easy. Mary had to make sure that she carried a pack of gum on her at all times to ensure that any time she felt stress, she would have a stick of gum to chew instead of biting her nails. Repetition is the key to success when it comes to habit transformation. If she found herself feeling stressed and didn't have any gum on hand, she would go right back to her old habit of biting her nails. But after a few months of straight repetition, she realized that she no longer had the desire to bite her nails. Slowly but surely, her gum habit had replaced her nail-biting habit. Not only did she now have beautiful nails, but she had dramatically decreased her risk of infection and had the additional benefit of fresh, minty breath (Sims, 2018).

Another example of a chronic, "hopeless" nail biter is Mandy (Duhigg, 2014). At just 24 years old, her nail-biting habit had become so bad that she would often gnaw away at her fingers until they bled. Many times, she would continue to bite her nails until they actually pulled away from the skin underneath. Her fingertips were covered in scabs, her fingers had become blunted and misshapen without nails to protect them, and she was beginning to feel tingles and sharp pains in her fingers, often a sign of nerve damage. In addition to compromising her health, Mandy's nail-biting habit had ruined her social life. She was so embarrassed around her friends that she kept her hands hidden away in her pockets, and found it nearly impossible to go on dates or meet new people. She had tried all the usual tricks, including painting her nails and dipping her fingers in lemon juice, but to no avail.

However, when the psychologist at her state university's counseling center asked her to complete the 3-step process, she was able to identify her habit loop. The cue, as it turned out, was boredom. The reward was not only distraction, but the physical sensation of her teeth biting her fingertips. The therapist suggested a replacement behavior that would satisfy this reward of experiencing some kind of light, physical sensation in her fingertips. She had to experiment with a few different behaviors, including putting her hands in her pockets or knocking on the desk every time she felt the urge to bite her nails. Finally, she found something that worked—rubbing her elbows with her fingertips. It sounds like an astonishingly simple solution to a problem that had caused so much physical and emotional distress in Mandy's life. But she would never have been able to come to that solution without first identifying her triggers and rewards. And she wouldn't necessarily have been able to come to that solution without first experimenting with other replacement behaviors.

Like Mary and Mandy, you may have to experiment with a few different replacement behaviors before you find one that works for you. Even after you've identified your habit loop, you may discover additional layers or nuances to your experience when you try certain replacement behaviors. Experimentation is part of the process. Remember to always be patient with yourself. Each attempt at a replacement routine will reveal more about you. It will give you clues as to how you developed this habit, and may even reveal certain things about what was going on in your life when the habit was first formed. Find ways to encourage yourself to commit to your new behavior, and if you can, engage other people in your transformation process so that they can encourage and support you as well!

Example Routines for Addictive Habits

Snacking and smoking are two compulsive habits that millions of contemporary people battle every day. Though there are thousands of potentially destructive habits, these two are commonly cited as habits that people want to break because they're noticeable, they cause a great deal of damage very quickly, and they are very difficult to stop.

Snacking, whether you're craving sweets, pastries, salty snacks, or even sugary drinks like soda, is a particularly common habit in our contemporary world because of the unprecedented access we have to junk food. In today's world, it's rare that you find yourself in a situation where you have no access to chips, chocolate, soda, ice cream, or something else that's loaded with sugar, salt, or fat. And even if you don't have access, all it takes is a quick trip to the convenience store or a walk across the street to the coffee shop to satisfy your craving.

Snacking is an excellent habit for demonstrating the power of the 3-step process because it's a very common habit that often comes with very surprising triggers. Too many people find it nearly impossible to curb their snacking habit because they assume that the trigger is hunger. It would only make sense, right? To curb their habit, they try unsuccessfully to replace the snack with healthy alternatives, only to find themselves lapsing back to their old ways within a few weeks.

To successfully curb a snacking habit, however, the key is not to replace the snack, but the behavior. It's only after applying the 3-step process that people come to realize that their snacking habit may not be cured by hunger at all. They may have begun snacking as a way to cope with feelings of depression, anxiety, boredom, and even as a form of procrastination. If your snacking behavior is helping you to relieve feelings of boredom or has become an excuse for you to take a break from difficult projects at work, then simply replacing the snack with a salad isn't going to satisfy. Instead, replacement routines like going for a walk, allowing yourself five minutes to scroll through social media, or even scheduling a 15 minute call with your friend at the same time that you usually find yourself snacking will all be far more effective replacement routines.

Smoking is another extremely common habit that

is notoriously difficult to break because of culturally assumed cues. While nicotine is a physically addictive substance, the cues that triggered the formation of the habit in the first place are rarely related to the nicotine itself. Often, nicotine addiction and the habit form side-by-side. The dependency on nicotine is a *symptom* of the habit, not its original cause. If you're going to successfully quit smoking, then replacing your cigarettes with nicotine patches or an extra cup of coffee isn't going to do the trick, because these strategies aren't addressing the environmental cues that trigger the need to smoke in the first place.

The need for the nicotine "buzz" is a common trigger for smokers, but the need for stimulation that nicotine satisfies often develops before the addiction. For this reason, many people have found that replacing their cigarettes with a cup of coffee is enough to successfully kick the habit. Caffeine is a completely different chemical, and so won't resolve your chemical dependency on nicotine. What it does do, however, is address the emotional cue that caused you to seek out cigarettes in the first place, and provide you with the reward of feeling "buzzed" in a much healthier way.

However, many smokers have found that their triggers have almost nothing to do with the chemical nature of the cigarette. For many, taking "smoke breaks" provided a sense of structure to their day, an opportunity to socialize with other smokers, or even an excuse to go outside for a few minutes every day.

For these people, anything from taking a walk to a quick set of push-ups to a social media break are effective replacement behaviors that help to satisfy the social or structural rewards that they once got from smoking cigarettes.

No matter what your habit is, these two examples neatly illustrate why knowing your cues is so important for successful habit transformation. Understanding the cue can help you to understand the reward. Sure, you get a bit of a buzz from your daily cigarette, but perhaps the reward that transformed it into a habit was the time you got to spend chatting with your coworker. Now that you're trying to quit, a piece of Nicorette might take care of your nicotine dependency, but it won't satisfy your need for social interaction. Until that need is satisfied, you'll find yourself craving a cigarette whenever you find yourself feeling lonely. To this end, texting a friend or going on social media might be a beneficial replacement routine that you can commit to in the long run. Perhaps you can make it a point to reach out to a friend or family member that you want to reconnect with every time you find yourself craving a cigarette. Not only would this replacement behavior satisfy the social rewards you once got from smoking, but it might help you to achieve other social goals related to having a better relationship with your family or reconnecting with old friends.

No matter how appropriate your replacement routine is, however, it's important to choose something that you believe will work. If you don't believe that you can successfully overcome your habit, then you'll start to subconsciously sabotage yourself with feelings of self-doubt. Remember, people who are relaxed and confident find themselves with much deeper reserves of willpower and motivation than people who aren't. The more you doubt your ability to change, the more vulnerable you will be to slip back into your old habits.

It's for this reason that working toward a specific goal can be such a powerful motivator. Other people have gone as far as to set themselves up with reward systems to motivate themselves to stick with their new habit. For example, if you're trying to replace watching TV at night with going jogging, you might want to find a step tracking app on your phone that monitors how many miles you jog. Once you've hit a certain number of miles, reward yourself with a purchase, vacation, or other treat for sticking with your new habit.

Give It Time

Be prepared for the reality that you may not find a good replacement right away. Try to have fun with the experimenting, and be open to learning more about your behaviors and their cues. Above all, make sure that you give the replacement habit enough time to take hold before you decide that it's not a good fit for you. No matter which replacement routine you choose, commit to it for at least two weeks. A new replacement behavior is almost always going to feel difficult or uncomfortable at first. For the first two weeks, try to pay attention to how well the chosen replacement behavior satisfies the rewards that you once got from the old habit. How easy is it to successfully complete your replacement behavior? Perhaps you need to simplify it a bit in order to make it easy to repeat. How easy is it for you to remember your replacement behavior? If you have to constantly remind yourself of the new behavior, then it might require some modifications in order to fit better into your current lifestyle.

As much as you can, try to choose a replacement behavior that mimics the physical motions of the old. For nail biters or smokers, replacement habits that put something in your mouth, like chewing gum or taking a sip of water from a water bottle, will be much easier to implement because they closely mimic the physical movement of bringing your fingers up to your mouth. If you're a compulsive online shopper, find another activity that you can do on the computer, like reading a blog, taking quizzes, or even learning a new skill. The less you have to change in order to implement your new habit, the easier it will be. The further removed your new habit is from the one you're trying to replace, the harder it will be to repeat it every single day, even if it satisfies the rewards you got from the old habit.

The best way to determine if your replacement

habit is effective or not is to keep a journal. For the next two weeks, record how many times you engaged in your old habit without successfully replacing it with the new habit. For example, on your first day of trying to replace your nail-biting habit with chewing gum, you may still find that you bit your nails 20 times throughout the day. But on day two, you only bite your nails 15 times, and by day three, you're down to 12. Keeping this kind of journal can be a great way to keep track of your progress, and it can help you to monitor whether or not your replacement routine is really working. If, after two weeks, you still find that you're biting your nails 12-15 times a day, then you may want to consider finding a new replacement routine. But if, in two weeks, you're down to biting your nails only 5-10 times a day, you know that your replacement habit is working. All you need to do now is keep going. If you repeat the act of chewing gum when you're feeling stressed or bored enough times, then you'll succeed in making it a habitual behavior.

No matter what habit you're trying to break, it probably took months or even years to form. It's unreasonable to expect yourself to reverse years of repetition in just a few weeks' time. Be patient with yourself and expect your progress to be slow. Keeping track of your progress is a good motivator because it's something to look back on when things start to feel difficult or frustrating. Remember also that the neural pathways that formed around your old habit will never fully disappear. Though you may be successful in permanently changing your old behaviors, it's hardly uncommon to find yourself craving a cigarette after years of being successfully clean, or driving to the convenience store for a tub of ice cream after years of being sugar-free. Lapsing back to your old behavior isn't a failure. It doesn't mean that you weren't disciplined enough or that your new routine isn't good enough. When watching your progress, don't punish yourself for all of the times that you repeat your old behavior. Instead, reward yourself for every time that you successfully complete the new behavior.

If you're trying to replace online shopping with doing yoga, for example, don't beat yourself up if you find yourself on a shopping spree. Instead, keep track in your journal of every single time you successfully complete a yoga routine. After a certain number of days, weeks, or months, reward yourself with something that you really want. This kind of a reward system is far more motivating than a punishment system because it gives you something to work toward. Think of the example of Lisa and her trip across the Egyptian desert. In order to make that trip, she told herself, she would have to go an entire year without smoking a cigarette. That's a total of 365. Every day that she broke and smoked a cigarette instead of going for a jog, she didn't spiral down into despair or beat herself up. That day just didn't count toward her 365. Whenever she found herself craving a cigarette, all she had to do was look at how many more days she had to remain smoke free before she could plan her trip to stiffen her resolve. You can set yourself up with a similar reward system to give yourself a similar level of motivation. And if you can do it together with another person or group of people who are trying to break a habit similar to yours, then so much the better. This kind of reward system is especially easy now with the plethora of free apps on the market that can help you track everything from steps taken to meals eaten to the number of times you go to the gym.

7

Be Consistent

There's no way around it — creating new habits takes both time and patience. Neural pathways aren't formed overnight, especially if you are over the age of 24. But each time you repeat the new behavior, that's one more link until the new pathway is formed. Think of it like a railroad track or a chain, with each repetition forming one more link in the new bridge you're building between your cue and your reward.

The day on which you need the most willpower to successfully perform your new routine is the first. Every single day that you successfully repeat the new habit makes it that much easier. If you can make it through the first day, you're far more likely to make it through the second. If you make it through the first two weeks, you're almost guaranteed to make it through the month. Unlike acquiring a new skill, which tends to increase in difficulty the more you learn, habit formation actually becomes easier over-

Creating New Habits

time. Whenever you're feeling frustrated or disappointed in yourself, remind yourself that this is as difficult as it gets. Habit formation is an all downhill climb. The most difficult step you'll take in your journey is the first one.

Once you've completed the 3-step process and chosen a suitable replacement behavior, the key ingredient is simple repetition. The more you do it, the more automatic it will become. Automaticity is essential for a behavior to become a habit, and repetition is essential for a behavior to become automatized (Schmidt & Retelsdorf, 2016). For the first few repetitions, focusing your willpower and self-control will be essential. The more disciplined you are, the more likely you are to commit to your new habit. However, the more successfully you repeat a behavior, the less willpower will be required to repeat the behavior again.

Inspiring yourself to make those first few, difficult repetitions is where setting a goal or tracking your progress comes in. Working toward a desired outcome will give you the inspiration you need to push through the first difficult weeks. The more automatic your new behavior becomes, you'll find yourself checking your progress less and less frequently. After a while, you won't have to think about it at all. Motivation will no longer be necessary to prompt you to engage in the new, beneficial behavior.

However, another strategy you can employ to improve your self-control in the beginning is to make small adjustments to your environment that will help you to remain committed to the new behavior. For example, if you're trying to lose weight by eating healthier food, you can employ strategies like using smaller plates when you cook or sitting with your back to the room when you go out to eat. The more temptations you can remove from your environment, the easier it will be to force yourself to make those first successful repetitions.

The occasional lapse back into your old behaviors can feel like a much bigger setback than it really is. A recent study measured the effects that one daily lapse back into an old habit has on the automaticity of the replacement habit (Lally et al., 2009). The study found that missing one day of repetition of a new routine had a negligible effect on how likely that person was to successfully complete the new routine the following day. To be specific, the study used a system of measurement that translated automaticity into a point system. The study found that every day that a new behavior was successfully repeated caused an increase in automaticity of .79 points. However, if a repetition was missed, their automaticity only went down to .55 points, a barely noticeable difference. Don't let a mere .24 point difference in automaticity discourage you to the point that you give up on your new routine! A relapse is far more damaging to our emotions and self-esteem than it is to our cognitive ability to form the new habit (Lally et al., 2009).

Studies have also shown us not to underestimate

the effects that our physical and social environments have on our habitual behaviors. One study showed that students were far more likely to successfully read the newspaper everyday if there were other students that were also reading the newspaper (Dean, 2013). Humans are inherently social creatures. We subconsciously want to feel like we're part of the group. If our new routine makes us feel included, we'll be more motivated to stick with it. It's for this reason that finding a partner or group to start your new routine with will make you far more likely to be successful at it. Depending on the nature of your replacement behavior, you can choose to find other people who are trying to transform the same destructive habit, or people who are trying to implement the same beneficial habit. For example, if you're trying to replace drinking with jogging, you can find a partner who's also trying to drink less, or you can find a partner who wants to start jogging every day. Either way, the social reinforcement that you get from the group will be a powerful subconscious motivator to stick with your new routine.

Another study attempted to determine how important willpower was in the formation of new habits (Wood, 2017). The study looked at participants who were trying to develop the habit of going to the gym. The study concluded that while motivation was very important in the beginning, those who successfully went to the gym every day for three months needed no motivation at all to continue going to the gym afterward. After just five weeks of repetition, the study found participants regularly attending the gym even in the face of environmental obstacles like surprise social opportunities or extra difficult days at work. The conclusion? Willpower is important to start a new routine, but by far, the most important factor in the formation of new habits is automaticity (Wood, 2017).

When Does A Habit Become a Habit?

The number of successful repetitions necessary before a behavior becomes a habit will greatly vary from person to person. Factors like how long the destructive behavior has been going on, exposure to environmental temptations, and how much social support you have can all combine to determine exactly how long you need to commit before your new routine becomes an automatic behavior.

However, there are a number of studies that show some loose trends in how long it takes for a behavior to become a habit. A recent behavioral study concluded that, depending on the nature of the habit and simplicity of the routine that's replacing it, a habit can take anywhere from 18 to 254 days of repetition to form, with an average of 66 days, or two months (Lally et. al., 2019). This is the same study that was able to conclude that one missed opportunity had almost no effect on the automaticity of a new routine. Based on this and other studies, it's

Creating New Habits

commonly accepted wisdom that, if you successfully repeat something 100 times, it's almost guaranteed to become a habit. When embarking on your own transformation process, it's reasonable to commit to two months of repetition before you can reasonably expect your new routine to become automatic.

Another way to track your progress is to make a note on your calendar every time you successfully repeat your new routine. Once you've reached 66 repetitions, then you can start to call your new routine a habit! Remember, one missed opportunity has almost no effect on the habit's automaticity, so your 66 days of repetition don't have to happen consecutively in order for your new habit to become automatized. If you miss a day, don't worry about it. It just means that your total journey is now going to be 67 days toward habit formation, with 66 days of repetition and one missed opportunity.

A fun way to motivate yourself to reach that 66-day mark is to set yourself a reward at the end. That way, when you do complete your 66 successful repetitions, you'll experience the double reward of knowing that you successfully integrated a new habit and the satisfaction of awarding yourself a prize for your achievement.

Remember, however, that some new habits took as long as 254 repetitions to become automatized, so at the end of your 66 days, if you're still struggling to complete your new routine, don't worry. By that point, you're already well on your way toward automaticity. You can still reward yourself because you know that, going forward, it will require far less willpower to complete future repetitions. If you like, you can set yourself another 66-day repetition challenge, with a similar reward at the end of your 66th day.

One clear trend that the study found was that simpler actions became automatized much faster than complex ones. When trying to start a new habit, the simpler you can make it, the easier it will be to successfully repeat, and the faster it will become neurologically engrained. Doing yoga at home on your laptop is going to be easier to make a habit than going to a physical studio, simply because you've removed the extra steps of getting in your car, battling traffic, and then driving yourself home. Not only are you more likely to repeat the action 66 successful times, but your brain will form the pathways faster because it will have less information to process with each repetition.

For similar reasons, the study also found that habits that closely mimicked the physical movements of the old habit formed much faster than habits that required different physical motions. Replacing drinking alcohol with doing push-ups, for example, is going to take more repetitions than replacing drinking alcohol with drinking water. The habitual motion of raising a glass to your lips is stored in your brain as part of the habit behavior. If you aren't requiring yourself to change that motion, then you can take advantage of the habitual infrastructure that's already formed in your brain when creating the new habit. Rather than having to do something else entirely, you'll only need to make the slight adjustment of pouring yourself a glass of water instead of an alcoholic beverage.

Another successful strategy I've seen is using three numbers indicated in the "66 days" study to monitor your progress from old habit to new (Lally et. al., 2009). Remember, this study was an attempt to monitor just how fast it actually takes for a habit to form. In this study, the simplest habits become automatic after just 18 days of repetition, so no matter how complex your habit may be, give yourself a reward after your 18th successful repetition. Consider that a benchmark. Then, after your 66th repetition, give yourself another reward, something slightly bigger. You're halfway there! Finally, when you've reached your 254th repetition, give yourself a big, dramatic congratulations. 254 days was the longest it took for an action to become a habit in this study. Your new habit may become automatized long before your 254th day, but if you commit to consciously marking your progress all the way to that point, you can be almost 100% sure that your new habit is firmly ingrained as an automatic process.

To make your journey even easier, there are a number of different apps out there that are specifically designed to help you track your progress when starting a new habit. Free apps like HabitBull even help you to track multiple habits at the same time, and can be easily synced with the calendar and fitness tracking programs on your laptop or mobile device. This way, you can track your progress and keep yourself motivated without having to create the *additional* new habit of recording your successful repetitions. Let technology help you to focus on successfully achieving your goals. When you've reached your benchmarks, it will feel really good to look back at the app's tracking program to see how much progress you've actually made.

It's All About Repetition

Anything you can do that will motivate you to stick with your new habit will be beneficial in the long run. You can use your benchmarks of 18, 66, and 254 repetitions to not only reward yourself, but to make small tweaks that might make repetition easier. After 18 days of trying to do yoga every day, you might conclude that yoga at night after you get home from work would be easier than doing it in the morning when you first wake up. From day 18 to 66, try changing the time that you do your yoga routine and see if that makes it easier to successfully complete. On day 66, evaluate again. Many times, it's not the replacement routine that's making it difficult to repeat, but some factor of your lifestyle or environment that you hadn't anticipated becoming a problem.

It's also important to remember that everyone's brains and personalities work a bit differently. Some people are better suited to strict routines than others. Some like their lives to be highly structured, while others prefer a bit of fluidity. There is nothing better or worse about having either of these lifestyle preferences, but they can affect your ability to successfully repeat a new behavior enough times to make it automatic.

If you google how long it will take you to form a new habit, you may see the number 21 pop up quite a bit. The popular myth that it only takes 21 days of repetition to form a new habit comes from a book called *Psycho-Cybernetics*, published in 1960 by Dr. Maxwell Maltz. In the book, Maltz himself doesn't suggest that 21 is enough for a new behavior to become a habit. Instead, he suggested this timeframe as a useful benchmark for both himself and his patients. Many, he found, had been able to successfully automatize their behaviors by this point. Even those who were still far from automatization, he found, required far less willpower to make successful repetitions after reaching this benchmark. If you want to use this benchmark to track your own progress, I highly encourage you to do so. But when beginning your transformation journey, expect that it is going to take you many more than 21 successful repetitions to fully automatize your new routine.

A study by the National Institutes of Health (NIH) concluded that pleasure based habits were by far the most difficult kind of habit to fully transform (Frothingham, 2019). Habits that provide you with a reward that is somehow pleasantly sensory in nature can be particularly difficult to let go of because it can be difficult to replicate the sensation with a replacement routine. Sensory pleasure also causes our brain to release a certain chemical called dopamine. This is often cited as the chemical that makes us "happy," and it is released most often in response to physical pleasures like sex, eating a delicious meal, petting a fluffy animal, or lying in a comfortable bed. Habits that end in a sensory reward also end in a dopamine rush, which is something that your brain doesn't give up lightly.

If your habit is related to some kind of sensory pleasure, you will find the most success if you replace it with another routine that releases a similar amount of dopamine. The appropriateness of these replacements will depend on the nature of the habit you are trying to break, but there are a few healthy behaviors that trigger the release of dopamine in the brain that can be effective substitutes for your destructive behaviors (Frothingham, 2019).

Protein

Proteins are made up of tiny building blocks called amino acids. When these amino acids are processed in the digestive tract, it gives the body a boost of energy. And that boost of energy feels good, so good that high protein meals can sometimes trigger a dopamine rush. Though it might seem strange, replacing a destructive eating habit with protein rich foods like turkey, beef, or legumes may trigger the same dopamine rush and therefore offer a similar reward to your old habit.

Exercise

Exercise is an incredibly powerful producer of a number of happy chemicals called "endorphins," only one of which is dopamine. This is good news for those who wish to implement a physical habit like walking, going to the gym, or generally exercising more. Even if exercise isn't high on your priority list, however, it can be a satisfying replacement for habits that yield sensory rewards.

Music

A number of studies have shown the power that music has over our brains. Listening to music that you enjoy feels so good because it triggers the release of dopamine. Replacing sensory or pleasure based habits with listening to music can be quite effective, especially with the access we have today to music streaming apps. If you like, you can even make yourself a habit transformation playlist that you can listen to whenever you feel the urge to engage in the old habit. To the same end, pairing music with your new routine can add an additional boost to rewards you receive from successfully completing the new routine. So, if you're trying to replace watching TV every night with study time, consider making a "study" playlist that you can listen to while you're working. Your brain will eventually come to associate the dopamine rush you get from listening to music with the act of studying, making it that much easier to successfully repeat your new routine.

Meditation

Believe it or not, many studies have linked the beneficial cognitive effects of meditation with increased dopamine levels in the brain. This kind of research suggests that not only could meditation be a satisfactory replacement for pleasure based habits, but it can come with the additional rewards of relaxation, improved cognitive ability, and even higher energy levels.

8

The Key Ingredient

...Is belief. Nothing can be done unless you believe that lasting change is possible. The founder of Alcoholics Anonymous recognized how powerful belief can be as a motivator, and this is the reason for the emphasis on religious faith in the traditional AA methods. Though the founder of AA publicly expressed his disdain for organized religion, he also understood that a strong belief in God could be an effective route for people to find belief in their own ability to change their behaviors. Believing in a higher power helped them to feel less guilty or responsible when they relapsed, and gave them positive cognitive thought patterns to replace negative feelings of depression or self-doubt.

Recent studies have confirmed that people are much more likely to lapse back into destructive habits after moments of stress, trauma, or frustration. One study of alcoholics, however, found that those with a strong sense of belief, whether it was in God, another religious philosophy, or simply in their own powers of resilience were significantly less likely to experience a relapse than those without a strong belief system (Duhigg, 2014). You don't have to start going back to church in order to cultivate a belief system. Faith in yourself is more than enough to see you through a particularly difficult habit transformation.

Belief is not a feeling, but a skill. Like any other skill, it takes practice to cultivate, especially if it's not something that you're used to. Though repetition is what automatically programs a behavior into the brain, human beings aren't robots. No matter how many years an alcoholic remains sober, and no matter how beneficial their replacement routines are, the new habits won't eliminate the reasons that person started drinking in the first place. Eventually they have a bad day, and the new routine isn't enough to convince them that everything is going to be ok. In that moment, the thing that prevents the alcoholic from reaching for a drink is the belief that they have the ability to cope with negative experiences without alcohol.

For many, the work of bolstering their belief is satisfied by becoming part of a community (Duhigg, 2014). On dark days, other members of your group can provide you with the support and encouragement that you can't seem to find within yourself. Just as humans are more likely to engage in behaviors that they see other people doing, we are also more likely to believe statements that we hear from other people. Telling yourself that you're good enough might not be enough to encourage you on low or difficult days, but if someone else tells you that you're good enough, that can often give you the boost you need to remain committed to your new routine.

Another benefit of community is the ability to watch other people succeed at overcoming the same challenge you've taken on yourself. You may not believe that a replacement routine will be enough to curb your habit, but watching other people do it successfully will provide you the evidence that you need. The more you see the same processes working for others, the more you'll start to believe that you, too, can succeed. When you experience moments of frustration, you'll also have examples that you can look to as role models, people whose stories can inspire you to push through your own moments of darkness and doubt. Groups often come with certain ingrained support structures, which can provide you with necessary coping mechanisms to help combat self-sabotaging thoughts.

Your "community" doesn't need to be a large group. Even one other person cheering you on can be enough to keep you feeling supported and empowered, especially if that person is someone you love like a good friend or a romantic partner. And your group doesn't necessarily have to be experiencing the same struggles or combating the same destructive habits in order to keep you inspired. In fact, a powerful way to motivate yourself to stick to a new routine is to join a group of people who are trying to implement the same new habit into their lives. Whether you're trying to read more often, study longer, or learn the piano, finding a group of people who are trying to do the same can be just as inspiring as joining a group of former alcoholics, smokers, or compulsive shoppers.

Wherever you get your stores of belief, it's a necessary ingredient for permanent change. Repetition and automaticity are powerful forces, but they can only get you so far. Belief is the difference between permanent change and a future relapse. Belief is your safety net when you run out of willpower or find yourself lacking the self-control you need to remain committed to your new routine. If you don't believe that what you're doing will work, then you'll be more vulnerable to self-sabotaging thoughts. One missed opportunity has almost no discernible effect on automaticity, but if you don't believe in yourself, that one missed opportunity can lead to feelings of frustration and low self-worth that ultimately knock you off course.

Sabotaging thoughts and feelings of doubt don't always come from within, however. As much as possible, distance yourself from other people who openly criticize or discourage you from committing to your new routine. People that want you to remain trapped by destructive habits are not people that you want in your life. And people who don't believe in your ability to successfully transform your life for the better aren't people that you want to spend much time with, either.

Creating New Habits

Though it isn't always possible to distance yourself from toxic friends and family, their negative energy and unsupportive attitude can be difficult for you to overcome. If there are people in your life that aren't supporting you, it can be even more important to find an encouraging community whose words can bolster you against the negative attitudes coming from other people in your life.

Conclusion

Bad habits can give us the horrible feeling of having no control over our own minds and bodies. Destructive habits always start out innocently, but they can have terrible long-term consequences for our physical health, mental wellness, social lives, and even our financial security. The power of destructive habits is very real for anyone who has attempted to overcome them. And while overcoming those habits is rarely easy, it's absolutely possible. Just because it's difficult doesn't mean that it can't be fun or rewarding as well.

The most common mistake that people made when approaching habit transformation is thinking that they can change their behaviors through the power of their will alone. While it may not be comforting to think of yourself as vulnerable to your brain's automatic processes, the reality is that willpower has nothing to do with engagement in destructive habits. If you've given up on changing

Conclusion

your habits in the past because you "just weren't motivated" or you "weren't disciplined enough," you now know that neither of those things were true. If you couldn't get yourself out of a bad behavior pattern through sheer willpower, it doesn't mean you're weak. It means you're human.

At this point, you now have all of the tools that you need to transform even the most deeply ingrained destructive habits. Your habit, like all habits, is part of a loop. Once you've employed the 3-step process, you'll have a clear idea of what your cues are, and what rewards you once gained from your destructive habits. Armed with this knowledge, you can then create for yourself a transformation plan to replace your destructive habit with a new routine that will turn your habit loop from one of destruction to one of positivity and empowerment.

Do you remember Lisa? The woman who committed to quitting her smoking habit before travelling across the Egyptian desert? Her habit transformation journey began with one simple step—quit smoking. But by replacing that one destructive habit with one new, beneficial habit (jogging), she was able to initiate a positive chain of events that transformed multiple areas of her life. As you notice your new routine becoming more and more automatic, you'll also start to notice all of the new, positive changes that one new habit has brought into your life. Goals that once seemed impossible will start to seem attainable. The possibility of transforming other negative habits

Conclusion

will seem far more exciting, and your new habit will bring you that much closer to living the life that you truly wanted to live.

With this book, you now have the power to take back control over your life. No longer do you have to let yourself be ruled by the automatic programming in your brain. No longer do you have to feel like somehow you just aren't as motivated or disciplined as other people. With this book, you have access to the practical steps you can take to make positive change in your life, as well as access to contemporary research to help you better understand how your habits were formed in the first place. All you need to do now is believe that you *do* have the power to change your life for the better.

References

References

Ainslie, G. (2016). Intertemporal Bargaining in Habit. *Neuroethics*, *10*(1), 143–153. https://doi.org/10.1007/s12152-016-9294-3

Chen, W., Chan, T. W., Wong, L. H., Looi, C. K., Liao, C. C. Y., Cheng, H. N. H., Wong, S. L., Mason, J., So, H.-J., Murthy, S., Gu, X., & Pi, Z. (2020). IDC theory: habit and the habit loop. *Research and Practice in Technology Enhanced Learning*, 15(1), 1–19. https://doi.org/10.1186/s41039-020-00127-7

Dean, J. (2013). *Making Habits, Breaking Habits* (First Trade Paper Edition). Da Capo Lifelong Books.

Duhigg, C. (2014) *The Power of Habit*. Penguin Random House.

Frothingham, S. (2019, October 24). *How Long Does It Take for a New Behavior to Become Automatic?* Healthline. https://www.healthline.com/health/how-long-does-it-take-to-form-a-habit#:%7E:text=It%20-

References

can%20take%20anywhere%20from,new%20behavior%20to%20become%20automatic.

Lally, P., van Jaarsveld, C. H. M., Potts, H. W. W., & Wardle, J. (2009). How are habits formed: Modelling habit formation in the real world. *European Journal of Social Psychology*, *40*(6), 998–1009. https://doi.org/10.1002/ejsp.674

Manson, M. (2019, May 5). *The Build a Better Life Course*. Mark Manson. https://markmanson.net/courses/build-a-better-life-course/build-a-better-life-course-learn-more

Mary Sims. (2018). *Habit Formation and Deconstruction: A Study in Behavioral Psychology*. https://digitalcommons.kennesaw.edu/cgi/viewcontent.cgi?article=1012&context=emergingwriters

Schmidt, Fabian T. C., & Retelsdorf, J. (2016). A New Measure of Reading Habit: Going Beyond Behavioral Frequency. *Frontiers in Psychology*, *7*, 1–8. https://doi.org/10.3389/fpsyg.2016.01364

Wood, W. (2017). *Basic Regulatory Processes*. University of Southern California.

Wood, W., & Rünger, D. (2016). Psychology of Habit. *Annual Review of Psychology*, *67*(1), 289–314. https://doi.org/10.1146/annurev-psych-122414-033417

Printed in Great Britain
by Amazon